Angela Rippon's West Country

ALSO BY ANGELA RIPPON

RIDING

MARK PHILLIPS: THE MAN AND HIS HORSES

VICTORIA PLUM (*for children*)

Angela Rippon's West Country

with photographs by Derry Brabbs

MICHAEL JOSEPH : LONDON

For you.
Because although this is
My West Country
It has so much that is worth sharing with others.

Contents

Near Two Bridges

First published in Great Britain by Michael Joseph Ltd
44 Bedford Square, London WC1B 3DU

ISBN 0 7181 2175 9

Printed and bound in Italy by Arnoldo Mondadori

My West Country

The world was a big place when I was four. It stretched so far to the east that it took all of half an hour to reach the Plymouth kindergarten, where I spent my days Monday to Friday, nine until four, clutching my mother's hand and jogging three steps to her one.

To the west of my kingdom lay the Royal Marine Barracks where my father served his King and country, while my northern boundary – Union Street – lay just the other side of the houses that joined onto our back yard. It was a place of noise and excitement. There were more pubs than grocers, every other shop let its goods spill out onto the pavement, and you could earn a penny by running errands.

Finally, on the southern border there was the sea. It lay just the other side of the grassy slopes of Plymouth Hoe. I could always smell it long before I ever saw it – a clean sharp tang carried on the south-westerlies that bounced off the coast and sneaked through the streets into the land-locked jumble of houses where we lived.

In 1948, Plymouth was not a pretty place. Five years of war had left it haggard and shell-shocked, and the bombing raids, graphically remembered as the Blitz, had ripped it apart, brick by brick. But at four, I saw none of the ugliness. Even the jagged remains of bomb sites were nothing more than vast adventure play-grounds for me and the rest of the children in the neighbourhood.

This then was my world. All two square miles of it, with invisible boundaries that to me were as real as any city wall. A small pudding basin of experience that left a whole world to discover as I grew up and grew older. Each year, I poked my head a little higher over the rim of the basin, and gave my world new horizons.

My father's stories of his journeys to China and Japan, New Zealand and America, were carefully traced across the blue-paint oceans of my tin globe. When I was seven, I got a bicycle for Christmas and, because it was too far to cycle to Japan, he and I settled for the South Hams instead.

Summer weekends became voyages of discovery – to the beaches of Bantham and Bigbury, through the slumbering villages of Brixton and Yealmpton. My Durham-born father was a countryman at heart and through his infectious delight in the countryside around him, I discovered, without ever having to learn, the flowers of the hedgerow, noted the flight pattern of birds, and recognised the leaf pattern of trees.

A short trip across the Tamar on the Torpoint Ferry, under the shadow of Brunel's curvacious railway bridge, gave us access to the south-eastern coast of Cornwall. The roads from Saltash and Torpoint to Kingsand and Cawsand were quartered and memorised and, when we moved to an estate on the edge of the city, I discovered that Dartmoor and all its wild beauty was on my doorstep.

There were walks through the shaded, narrow paths in Lydford Gorge to the spectacular waterfall where the overflow from moorland streams drops a hundred feet between boulders and ancient trees into the arms of the River Lyd. And picnics by the quiet upper reaches of the River Dart where it twists a carefree path between soft moorland hills below Hexworthy and Holne Moor.

I'd never seen valleys more beautiful, nor hills so noble. They seemed to stretch to eternity, offering not one but a dozen horizons. A landscape coloured by the purple of heather, the vibrant yellow of gorse. Mottled by the light and shade of scudding clouds and patterned

Bliss at Duckpool; the two bridges crossing the Tamar

by the tracery of low stone walls, marking the boundary of 'new take' – fields where Dartmoor farmers have gradually tamed the unkempt moor into working land.

There were mornings when the moorland turf was hung with delicate strands of silver cobwebs, as if the spiders had spun a million washing-lines. And evenings when the moon disappeared behind black clouds, leaving only the lights of isolated villages to glow like pearls on night velvet.

It was then that I grew to love Dartmoor more than any other place on earth. To develop, I suppose, an unashamed love affair with a landscape that I would one day make my home, for when my husband, Chris, and I found our house on the edge of Dartmoor near the town of Tavistock, we both knew we'd come to a place neither of us would ever want to leave. But that was still very much in the future. As a young girl, Dartmoor was only one small part of a West Country that still held much for me to discover.

Holidays in north Cornwall revealed the power of Atlantic breakers crashing onto the beach at Bude and rolling with slightly less ferocity across the golden sands of Polzeath.

In north Devon, we lazed on the endless beach at Instow, and slept in an old green caravan that was gently rocked and nudged each night as the sheep who shared

Rural life near Hexworthy

the field with us crept underneath for shelter.

As a junior reporter on the local Sunday newspaper, I ventured deeper into previously unknown territory at the wheel of my very first car – an ancient, much loved Morris Eight series E, christened Deborah, or Debbie for short, from the letters of her registration, DBO 768 – always meeting new people, finding new haunts.

Some of the most pleasant – and certainly laziest – days were spent on the banks of the River Yealm in south Devon, reporting on the activities of the local sailing club. Sitting in the sunshine, with the twin villages of Newton Ferrers and Noss Mayo on either side, and the blue ribbon of water winding down through tree-lined banks towards the English Channel and the Mew Stone, it was difficult to remember sometimes that I was actually working for a living!

But it wasn't until I became a television reporter in 1966 that my pudding basin finally shattered, and the whole of the south-west peninsula was opened up to me.

The words of Daphne du Maurier in books like *Frenchman's Creek* and *The King's General* had painted pictures in my mind of the Helford River, but it was a day's fishing with the oystermen of Porth Navas that finally brought that lovely river to life. While on Exmoor, I chased the ghost of Lorna Doone; and, at Appledore, the centuries were rolled away for me by Joe and Oswald Bennett, two brothers in their late seventies. Their skill with ropes and rigging belonged to an age when sail, not steam, powered ships.

It is certainly one of the bonuses of being a reporter that through my work I've met some of the great characters and craftsmen of the region. People who, in turn, have introduced me to their special places in the West Country. Like ninety-one-year-old Frank Webber, his junior colleague, Percy Brooks (a mere lad of seventy-four!) and their young mate, Fred Hill – aged seventy. Three men who cut peat and granite out of the moor above Okehampton. And Ron Delderfield, that craftsman with words, whose circular study looked

Daphne du Maurier country : the Helford River

down on the pretty houses and neat seafront of Sidmouth.

For seven years, my work took me from Lynton to Honiton, Penzance and Barnstaple, and many points in between. Landmarks on the skyline became as familiar as my own back garden. The clay tips of St Austell, with their white, geometric moonscape peaks rising up out of the green countryside, the spires of Truro Cathedral, the massive tower of its counterpart in Exeter; the tall grain tower in the farm beyond Hatherleigh that for me marked the half-way point across the county of Devon, and the distinctive coastline of cliffs and ploughed fields that welcomed me across the border from Somerset into Devon on the northern coast.

Each day offered the pleasure of discovery or renewed acquaintance. Sometimes, the demands of a news story meant that the countryside passed me by in a hectic blur, but there were occasions when I could take a detour to explore a new valley or stretch of coastline, perhaps even steal half an hour to walk over familiar turf and drink in the clean air and stunning views from a favourite corner of my ever-expanding countryside.

And, as a 'local TV personality', the invitations to 'come to a barn dance at Colyton' in east Devon, or to 'open a garden fête near South Molton', even 'be chairman of a musical evening in Redruth' and a hundred and one other occasions, have left me with memories guaranteeing that not one of those places will ever be just another name on the map.

So what is *my* West Country? Well, for a start, it doesn't take in any part of Somerset or Dorset, nor follow the nooks and crannies of an authorised map of Devon and Cornwall, for there are still towns and villages I've never visited, roads and lanes that remain uncharted.

My West Country is exactly that – a collection of places that are personal to me after a lifetime of living and working in the region. It's the area where I was born, the people and places that helped me grow from adolescent to adult, weaving their influence and imagery into the very pattern of my life.

There are places I've omitted, simply because time and space simply don't allow me to include every milestone and memory in my life. Places also, no doubt, that are favourites of your own, places that are for you the very essence of the West Country. But then that's what makes them *your* West Country – not mine.

Within these pages are the places where my roots are – that's what makes it my West Country.

A moonscape of clay tips near St Austell and, in total contrast, two North Devon rural scenes – near Hartland Point and Exmoor

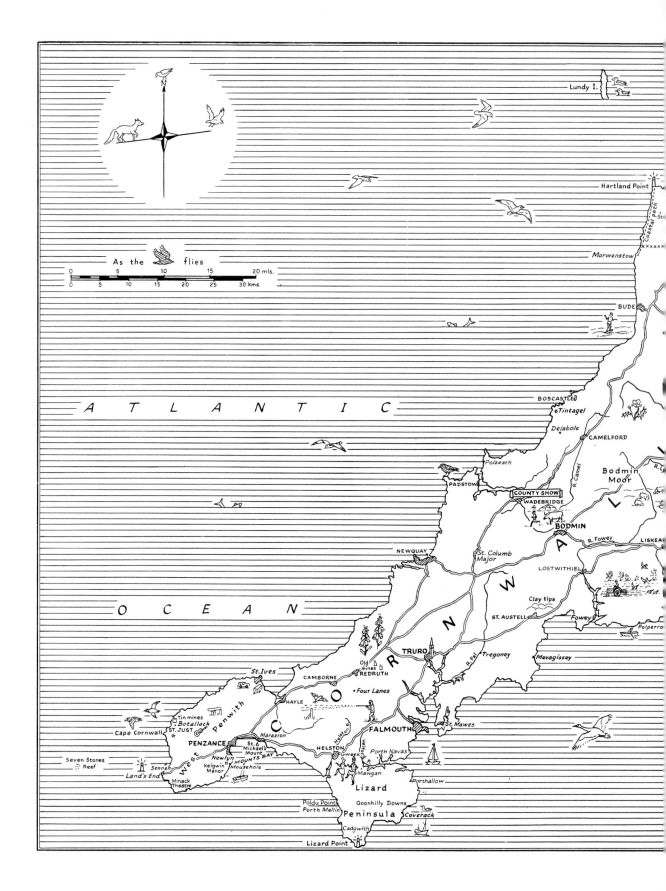

Lundy I.

Hartland Point

Coastal path

Morwenstow

As the ← flies

0   5   10   15   20 mls.
0   5   10   15   20   25   30 kms.

BUDE

A   T   L   A   N   T   I   C

BOSCASTLE
•Tintagel
Delabole
CAMELFORD

Bodmin
Moor

Polzeath

PADSTOW

R. Camel

R.

COUNTY SHOW
WADEBRIDGE

BODMIN

LISKEA

R. Fowey

NEWQUAY

St. Columb
Major

LOSTWITHIEL

O   C   E   A   N

W   A   L

Clay tips

ST. AUSTELL

Fowey

Polperro

TRURO

R. Fal   Tregoney

Mevagissey

Old
mines
REDRUTH

St. Ives

CAMBORNE

C   O   R   N

Four Lanes

HAYLE

Tin mines
•Botallack
ST. JUST

West Penwith

C   O

Cape Cornwall

PENZANCE

Marazion

St. Michael's
Mount

FALMOUTH

St. Mawes

Seven Stones
∴ Reef

Sennen

Newlyn
MOUNTS BAY
Keigwin
Manor
Mousehole

HELSTON

Gweek

Porth Navas

Land's End

Minack
Theatre

Lizard

Mawgan

Porthallow

Poldu Point
Porth Mellin

Goonhilly Downs
Peninsula   Coverack

Cadgwith

Lizard Point

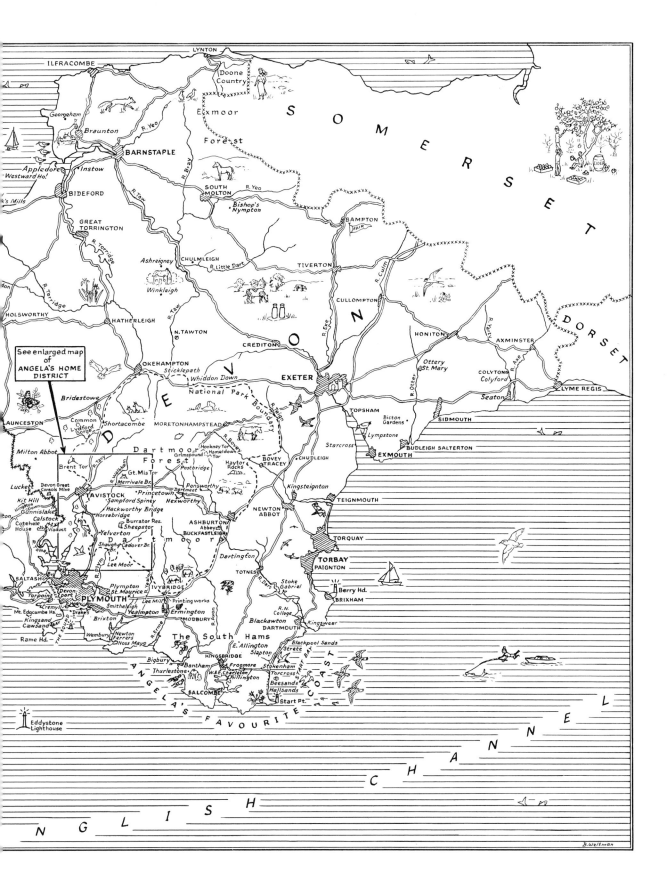

ILFRACOMBE

LYNTON

Doone
Country

Exmoor

Forest

S O M E R S E T

Georgeham

Braunton

R. Yeo

BARNSTAPLE

R. Bray

Appledore
Westward Ho!

Instow

SOUTH
MOLTON

R. Yeo

's Mills

BIDEFORD

R. Taw

Bishop's
Nympton

BAMPTON
FAIR

GREAT
TORRINGTON

R. Torridge

Ashreigney

CHULMLEIGH

R. Little Dart

TIVERTON

D O R S E T

R. Torridge

R. Taw

Winkleigh

CULLOMPTON

R. Culm

HOLSWORTHY

HATHERLEIGH

R. Exe

N. TAWTON

HONITON

AXMINSTER

R. Yarty

don

CREDITON

O

N

Ottery
St. Mary

R. Axe

COLYTON
Colyford

See enlarged map
of
ANGELA'S HOME
DISTRICT

OKEHAMPTON
Sticklepath
Whiddon Down

EXETER

R. Otter

Seaton

LYME REGIS

Bridestowe

National Park Boundary

D

R. Teign

Topsham

Bicton
Gardens

SIDMOUTH

LAUNCESTON

Common
Lydford
Gorge

Shortacombe

MORETONHAMPSTEAD

E

R. Bovey

Lympstone

BUDLEIGH SALTERTON

Milton Abbot

Brent Tor

Hookney Tor
Grimspound
Hameldown
Tor

V

Starcross

EXMOUTH

Luckett

R. Tavy

Dartmoor

Forest

Postbridge

Haytor
Rocks

CHUDLEIGH

Devon Great
Consols Mine

Gt. Mis Tor

O

BOVEY
TRACEY

Kit Hill

Merrivale Br.

Princetown

Dartmeet
Ponsworthy

Kingsteignton

TAVISTOCK

Hingston
Down
Gunnislake

Sampford Spiney

N

Hexworthy

TEIGNMOUTH

Calstock

Hackworthy Bridge
Horrabridge

Burrator Res.

ASHBURTON
Abbey
BUCKFASTLEIGH

NEWTON
ABBOT

Cotehele
House

Viaduct

Yelverton

Sheepstor

D

Tame

Shaugh
Br.

Cadover Br.

a

r

t

m

o

o

r

Dartington

TORQUAY

SALTASH

Lee Moor

Dartmoor

Devon-
port

Plympton
St. Maurice

IVYBRIDGE

Lee Mill

TOTNES

R. Dart

Stoke
Gabriel

TORBAY
PAIGNTON

Berry Hd.

PLYMOUTH

Torpoint
Cremyll

Drake's

Smithaleigh
Brixton

Yealmpton

Printing works

Ermington
MODBURY

R.N.
College

BRIXHAM

Kingswear

Mt. Edgcumbe Ha.

Kingsand
Cawsand

Wembury

Newton
Ferrers
Noss Mayo

Blackawton

DARTMOUTH

Rame Hd.

The South Hams

E. Allington
Slapton

Blackpool Sands
Strete

Bigbury
Thurlestone

Bantham

KINGSBRIDGE

Frogmore
W.& E.Charleton
Chillington

Stokenham
Torcross
Beesands
Hallsands

START BAY

SALCOMBE

Start Pt.

THE SOUND

ANGELA'S

FAVOURITE

COAST

Eddystone
Lighthouse

E

N

G

L

I

S

H

C

H

A

N

N

E

L

B. Weltman

Plymouth: THE HOE

It's a pity that we don't remember or appreciate the things done for us as babies. If we could, I'd be pleased to cast my mind back to the summer of 1945 when the sun scattered sequins across the waves and a battered, victorious British Fleet plied in and out of Plymouth Sound.

Every afternoon that summer, my grandfather would march me across the broad tarmac esplanade of Plymouth Hoe, park my pram on the grass, and watch the naval comings and goings while I gurgled, burped and slept. It was from here that Drake is said to have carried on playing a nonchalant game of bowls while the Spanish Armada advanced up the Channel. The army generals fussed and fumed, expecting an invasion at any minute. But that wily old sea dog Drake knew every twist and turn of the winds and currents along the shore and reckoned that the Spanish sailors would battle for hours to gain just a few leagues against an outgoing tide and offshore wind. When he was ready, and the elements were in his favour, Drake set sail, routed the Armada and – well – the rest is history.

Drake still looks out across the waves from a vantage point on the Hoe, his hand resting lightly on his sword. Cannon and shot at the ready. But his Tudor finery, beautifully barbered beard, and steady eye are sealed in bronze. The statue is a replica of one that stands in the centre of a traffic island in his birthplace, Tavistock, fifteen miles away on the edge of Dartmoor. There he looks down on an avenue of houses, surrounded by cars and carbon monoxide. On the Hoe, he faces seaward, the salt still strong in his nostrils, and his gaze taking in the sweep of the Channel and the scene of his most famous sea battle.

No doubt, Grandfather often re-created those events in his mind, glorying in the spectacle of the chunky, butter-tub little men o'war under acres of white wind-filled sails, for he'd spent the greater part of his working life as a master sail maker in Devonport Dockyard, in an age when steam and diesel powered the ships, so that his own skills were limited to making canvas bags and hammocks, and the occasional sail for a yacht. As

View across the Sound which Sir Francis Drake will have seen before setting out on his most famous sea battle

Grandfather's silent companion on those occasions, I may not have shown much interest in the sea and the cliffs around me, but they undoubtedly left an impression on my subconscious for, like every native-born Plymothian, I've since spent hours on the grassy slopes and rocky 'beaches' of Plymouth Hoe looking out on the Sound and I am always proud to show it off to visiting friends and relatives.

The Hoe is a chunky outcrop of limestone that rises in an almost sheer wall, 110 feet out of the sea. It forms one side of a square that has the cliffs of Staddon Heights on one side, the gentle sweep of the Cornish border lands on the other, and the English Channel straight ahead. There's a kind of geometric neatness to the layout with the River Plym (from which Plymouth takes its name), making a sedate entry into the Sound from the top left-hand corner, while the River Tamar slices in from the right, its broad highway of water forming the boundary between Devon and Cornwall, and providing a sheltered deep-water harbour for the naval dockyard.

The original town of Plymouth was built in the lee of this huge lump of 'hoe' rock, in the area now called the Barbican. Elizabethan houses, cobbled streets and the lively fish market, combine to make this not just the oldest but also the most picturesque part of Plymouth. It was always a good place to rummage for antiques and fancy 'junk' and now boasts some of the finest fish restaurants in the county.

As Plymouth grew, the town expanded out onto the flat plane of land behind the Barbican, sheltering behind the vast bulk of the Hoe which acted like a giant weatherbreak.

King Charles II built an imposing army citadel on its heights, more to impress the local populace and keep them in order than to protect them, but apart from that one building, the Hoe was left intact for the Victorians and Edwardians to develop as a place of recreation.

The topmost ridge is covered with sloping lawns, shrubs that hang onto the banks by their fingertips and

The Naval Dockyard on the banks of the river Tamar

The picturesque Barbican, with an Elizabethan doorway

formal flower beds. In the days when I worked at a television studio in the city, I walked my old basset hound Plod along the Hoe every lunchtime for two years. From January to December, I could watch the four seasons change through the skills of the gardeners in the city's Parks department. Wallflowers and polyanthus every spring, roses and a riot of annuals throughout the summer, shrubs that gloried in the rich burgundy and gold of autumn hues, and in the winter the heathers and late-flowering shrubs that carried on regardless of the December gales and rain.

The face of the cliff is split in two by the gentle sweep of a road called the Esplanade. There are numerous paths that zig and zag through the shrubs down onto the pavement, and also a glorious example of architectural whimsey, known by all the 'locals' as The Wedding Cake – because that's exactly what it looks like. The semicircular balconies stride down the hillside, topped with balustrades fronted by elegant pillars and flanked by a cascade of steps. The graffiti artists have a field day on the great expanse of creamy, curved walls and supports. Scholars might trace the fortunes of the local football team (Plymouth Argyle), the love life of one half of the navy, and the parentage of the rest until, that is, the council moves in to re-paint the walls, and provide a clean canvas for a whole new chapter.

On summer evenings in the mid 1950s, it seemed as though half the population of the city turned out to promenade up and down the Esplanade watching small yachts scudding ahead of the wind, or being entertained by the young men who plunged off the high diving boards into the sea. No one ever thought they were showing off, and the more daring or complicated dives were rewarded with bursts of spontaneous applause and cheers from those of us who hung over the railings from the roadside to watch them.

Perhaps the most exciting views from those railings were not of people, however, but machines. The great Sunderland flying boats used to sweep in from the English Channel, circle overhead and then land in a jet stream of sea spray right in the middle of the Sound. The noise was deafening but the sight spectacular.

Below the Esplanade, the cliffs meet the sea, and although there's no beach to speak of, the whole place is crowded with swimmers and sunbathers in the summer. For the cliffs are laced with concrete terraces and jettys fused onto the rock, giving access to the sea, with a massive circular swimming pool as a centrepiece.

I got to know those sun terraces very well during my last few years at grammar school, which was barely a fifteen-minute walk from the shore. During the summer before I took my mock 'O' levels, I spent almost every sunny lunchtime squeezed into my own special corner, revising for examinations and sunbathing at the same time. Among the girls in my class, there was something of a competition every year to see who could get the deepest suntan. A lotion of olive oil and vinegar was the favourite tanning aid. It stank to high heaven, but fried you beautifully. The main disadvantage was that it left school text books smelling of stale fish and chips, but you soon learnt to put up with that, and anyhow by winter it had faded – along with the tan.

My special spot was a small hole in the rock close to one of the jettys, from where you could flop into the sea to cool off from the heat of the midday sun. The base of the hole was just large enough to take my bottom, while the rock face made a perfect slope for my back, and natural table for the books. It was perfect, and I regarded anyone who beat me to it as an intruder. A few years ago I reclaimed my spot to while away a few hours in the sun – and found it was unbelievably uncomfortable. Did I really sit there for hours with the rock poking into my back, and my rear end going numb against the hard ground, soaking up Tudor history and sunlight?

Ah well, times change. But remarkably the Hoe doesn't. Perhaps it's because there's a solid unyielding permanence to rock that it hasn't changed at all. The rest of the city has been rebuilt and renovated, and certainly Drake would hardly recognise it, but the Hoe looks exactly the same to me now as it did all those years ago.

Colourful flower beds on the Hoe ; 'The Wedding Cake' and the high-diving boards, a source of much entertainment

THE ROYAL MARINE BARRACKS

I doubt very much that the men who built the Royal Marine Barracks in 1781 intended the parade ground to be used as a children's playground. But in the years immediately after the last war, that's just what it became. Not entirely, of course. The band still marched tunefully up and down, backwards and forwards, and warrant officers rasped at lines of khaki-clad 'bootnecks' to 'qui-i-ck march' and 'ah-ten shun'. The sounds ricochetted off the four walls of the barrack square, catching the squaddies in the crossfire of command and counter-command, bludgeoning them under the sheer weight of decibels into the finest parade troops in the land. Not one head out of line, a miracle of human geometry.

But while all this was going on in the centre of the square, on the pavement around the perimeter, the children of the regiment played out their own lives.

At least two of the barrack blocks were partly divided into flats to house regimental families, and although my parents always lived in 'civvy street', I had a cousin living inside the square, and that made me acceptable as one of the barrack gang.

We played all the usual street games of skipping and hopscotch, hanging upside down on the ornamental railings, or aping our parents by sitting on the stone steps outside the flats and gossiping. In one corner of the square, a steep ramp connected the parade ground with the streets that ran on a lower level behind the main buildings. The angle of the slope and the sharp bend at the bottom were custom-made for trolley racing, and it wasn't long before we invented a particularly evil – and dangerous – game of 'chicken' in which this miniature tarmaced version of the Cresta Run played a vital part. If you rolled down the slope with your feet sticking over the side of the trolley, to act as brakes, you were 'chicken' – a title you had to live with until you were brave enough to hurtle down without brakes and only jerk the bits of string that steered the front wheels at the very last minute, so that you cruised along on the flat in front of the old wash houses, instead of splattering into the wall.

We also risked getting a clip round the ear, for it was one of the few exploits of which our parents disapproved. But even if the trolley run was occasionally put out of bounds for a while, the buildings still offered a maze of tunnels and roads, open spaces and secret places that made it a magical world for children, whose very presence helped to strengthen the feeling that still exists within the regiment – that it's more than just a body of fighting men, it's a very special family.

One of our favourite 'secret' places was the Drummers' Pit, a scoop of land, facing the sea, on the perimeter of the barracks where the famous Royal Marine Corps of Drummers were sent to practice when the rest of the unit couldn't stand the noise any longer. The solid rock of this natural amphitheatre could soak up the rattle of a dozen drummers and the prattle of fifty children – and the rest of the barracks wouldn't even know they were there.

I don't think you could ever say the barrack square is 'beautiful', but there's certainly a softness that almost, but not quite, rates as elegance, in the grey limestone and granite mullions of the main barrack buildings of Stonehouse. A row of lime trees along the pavement makes it look almost suburban. When the leaves turn transparent green in the sunlight, if you half-close your eyes, you might *almost* imagine you were standing in front of a Regency terrace. The two clock towers on either side of the arched entrance used to be covered in virginia creeper, which meant that every summer it looked as though the towers had been fashioned from an exotic shrub by an artist of topiary, rather than a stonemason.

The Ministry of Works stripped off the creeper some years ago. It's cleaner now and the offices don't get infested with snails and other crawling things but I still can't look at those towers without painting in the foliage in my mind's eye.

Happily, one bit of greenery the men from the Ministry have left well alone is a fine old chestnut tree. It stands just a few feet from the main entrance to the parade ground, outside the front door of what used to be the

The Royal Marine Barracks, and the fine chestnut tree where my father stood 'guard duty over the conkers'

Commanding Officer's residence. The tree grows safely inside the green railings – but its branches lean out over the spikes, weighed down each autumn with a bumper crop of conkers.

My father tells me that one morning he was told to report to the C.O.'s house at 11.30 a.m. He arrived in immaculate blue uniform, toe caps glinting, his Sam Browne belt supple and shining, and peak cap the regulation height above his nose – absolutely petrified. On the long march across the parade ground, he was trying to work out what he'd done to warrant a personal summons from the senior officer. When he arrived at the house, he was shown around to the front door, which opened out onto the street, and told to 'stand guard duty over the conkers'. Apparently every lunchtime and afternoon, when the children turned out of the local school, the tree was being raided for its hard glossy fruits and its branches were being snapped off in the process. So with all the solemnity that only the military can muster on these occasions, my father, and a rota of Royal Marines after him, was put on Conker Guard. Maybe that's why the tree has survived!

DEVIL'S POINT

I recently met a man who told me that, as a boy during the war, he could be swimming off the rocks at Devil's Point when the air raid siren started, get dressed – though probably not dried! – run the length of Durnford Street and be inside his home in Stonehouse before the last note of the siren had faded. Like me, he lived in a street called Emma Place that sits on the fringe of Plymouth's city centre. And also, like me, he simply took it for granted as a child that it was possible to live in a city environment and yet have the sea as our playground, as much as the streets and bomb sites around us.

It wasn't until I grew up and visited other seaports and cities that I realised how lucky I'd been. People who live in beach resorts or even fishing communities have an unquestioned access to the sea. But most cities which boast a commercial port or naval dockyard have had to surrender much of their shoreline to wharves and cranes and the jumble of dockland. Plymouth's rocky coast, however, made that monopoly impossible and created a sort of geological compromise with the Dockyard settled comfortably on flat ground a mile or so from the mouth of the Tamar, and the commercial port inconspicuously tucked into one of the deep-water coves, leaving acres of shoreline untouched, including that unpretentious lump of rock in the western corner – Devil's Point.

You won't find it marked on any tourist map as a recommended beach or bathing spot. In fact, it's a place that many Plymothians tend to think of as 'theirs' – and definitely out of bounds to visitors. In the depths of winter, it can look neglected and scruffy; in high summer, off-puttingly over-crowded. But it was here that I learnt to swim, where as children we'd stretch out on the rocks like lizards in the sun and where I wove dreams and fantasies that took me across the unknown blue of the ocean.

The point is at the very end of one of those old city streets that has known Georgian elegance, the ignominy of post-war depression and, more recently, the attentions of developers as an 'in' place to live. Durnford Street is lined with tall, narrow, plain-fronted houses, a façade which belies their real beauty and proportions. It's not unless you walk around to the back of the buildings that you begin to appreciate just why they're now among the most sought-after houses in the city.

They stretch down towards the sea with pretty bay windows often fashioned from curved timbers taken from the prows of old wooden sailing ships that were broken up in the yards two hundred years ago. The view from each window is virtually the same: a calm stretch of water timbered with the slender masts of sailing boats moored along the marina on the opposite shore, with a backdrop of Cornish hills beyond.

From halfway along, it looks as though Durnford Street comes to a dead end at a high stone wall and it isn't until you drive almost to its very foot that you see the road snakes around to the right, cutting a path between *two* walls. Palm trees and oak still grow in unlikely harmony behind the wall on the left, forming an effective curtain of foliage around what was Nazareth House orphanage.

But the wall on the right – that was a mystery. It towered up thirty feet, a mixture of stone and natural rock covered in ivy, and sprouting evergreens from somewhere on the other side. It was too high to climb – for me at least – and it wasn't until last year that I discovered what lay over the top.

It holds a magical garden that plays hide-and-seek behind hedges and trees, around lawns and through gates for an unbelievable two acres. And in the middle

sits a beautifully restored Georgian family house. When I finally got inside, just over a year ago, I felt like Mary discovering the Secret Garden. It had taken me years longer than Frances Hodgson-Burnett's young heroine, but my pleasure and the joy of discovery were just the same.

Nevertheless, I'm glad I didn't visit the garden as a small girl. If I had, it would have taken away the satisfaction of fantasy. For when you don't know what really lies behind a wall, your imagination can run riot!

Beyond that secret garden, the road suddenly opens out to reveal a small tower from where we bought ice creams and hired deck chairs, a low wall to stop people falling over the edge, and beyond that the sea – with the solid black conical mass of Drake's Island silhouetted against the skyline, looking as though it could almost be within touching distance. The tarmac path slips away to

The swimming pool at Devil's Point, and Durnford Street

the left across the top of the rocks, following the boundary wall of Nazareth House. This now houses an old people's residence run by a group of gentle, dedicated nuns. It's a modern block of red brick, attractively designed with large picture windows, sun balconies and arches which make it look more like an exclusive Mediterranean hotel complex rather than a charitable institution, and it certainly bears no resemblance to the building that stood there in the days when this was my old stomping ground.

The site originally belonged to the Mount Edgcumbe family whose main home still lies directly across the water on the Cornish shore in Mount Edgcumbe Park. At Devil's Point, they built their winter palace. A house of gracious proportions with massive windows that looked out over that glorious view and meant they could keep a weather eye on the family seat across the way!

Between the wars, the house was sold, and eventually passed to the nuns of Nazareth House who filled it with love and laughter and a whole gaggle of orphaned girls. On Sunday afternoons, the older girls would sit in those spacious picture windows, framed in true romantic style with leafy boughs, wearing their white confirmation frocks tied with huge satin sashes. From the outside looking in, how I envied their pretty dresses and their beautiful home. It didn't ever occur to me that from the inside looking out they might have envied me for having parents.

The small square swimming pool that's built straight onto the rocks at sea level is flushed and has its water changed on every high tide. Nowhere is it deeper than three foot, and that made it the perfect place to learn to swim as you could keep one foot on the bottom, while looking wonderfully efficient on the surface. The seniors, who must have been all of eight or nine, not surprisingly regarded the tiny pool as the place for babies and swam instead off the rocks straight into the sea. It was the ambition of every 'littley' to join the seniors, but I'm afraid I never graduated to that elite bunch. My parents moved house when I was seven, and Devil's Point became just another memory.

THE PALACE THEATRE

When she was barely sixteen, my grandmother ran away from her strict, Calvinistic family in Edinburgh to 'go on the stage'. One of her brothers finally spotted her in the chorus of a London show and she was dragged back to Scotland, harbouring unfulfilled ambitions – and a musquash fur coat. (We never did find out where she got it!) Eventually she was safely married off to a respectable southerner – my grandfather – and settled down to running a home and producing six children.

My memory of her is quite clear. Her hair was always secured in a neat, disciplined bun, the lyle stockings were never crumpled above polished buttoned shoes and the ubiquitous floral, wrap-around pinny was spotless. She was by all outward appearances, just another contented mother and grandmother who'd slipped comfortably from middle to old age. But the ample bosom beneath that pinny still concealed a passion for the theatre. So perhaps it's not surprising that the stage of the old variety house, the Theatre Royal, should be a few hundred yards from our front door, and that the building which straddled the end of our street was the lavishly ornate Palace Theatre.

Occasionally, Grandmother provided lodgings for the theatre company. She didn't have the stars to stay, her guests were usually out of the chorus, or the names on the bottom of the bill. But they breathed greasepaint and glamour into her home – and she came alive in the atmosphere.

When I was old enough to be trusted to sit still and not fidget for two hours, my weekly treat was a trip to the Palace. If Gran was flush, we'd both sit in the stalls. But if the pennies were a bit scarce, she would sit in the stalls alone and I'd be sent up into the cheapest seats in the gods – and threatened with all sorts of dire Highland oaths if I didn't meet up with her at the stage door minutes after the curtain came down.

Every visit was an adventure, and Grandmother's joy in the place was infectious. I didn't bother about what show we were to see – just being there was a treat.

Like so many of its contemporary buildings, the Palace looked like a theatre should. It had glamour and opulence, with a touch of whimsy. The outside was clad in shiny brown tiles, with two massive picture panels of Drake and the Spanish Armada. Dozens of small lights, trying to imitate hand braziers, glowed along the walls of the foyer and invitingly took you up the main staircase to the first floor lounge, where potted ferns and loom chairs lurked behind enormous pillars and a set of vast, copper cauldrons stood glowing from the loving attentions of the cleaning staff.

Inside the auditorium, it was all red plush velvet and golden cherubs. For a while during the sixties, the building was turned into a bingo hall, and 'brightened up' with purple and yellow paint. In recent years, the Palace has happily been rescued and, on limited funds, restored. Unfortunately, the rape of the sixties has left its mark, and the old girl has managed to reclaim only some of her dignity, but at least she's back to being a theatre again, a place where Pantomime and Variety put colour and laughter into people's lives, and that has to be a step in the right direction.

My early visits to the theatre were spiced with the privilege of sometimes being allowed back-stage because of my family's rather tenuous link with the performers. The touring casts of *Brigadoon* and *Oklahoma* became almost as familiar to me as the hit tunes they sang. And after watching my heroine, Beryl Grey, dance the lead in *Swan Lake*, I almost died with pride when I was allowed to stand outside her dressing room, and read her name

The Palace Theatre looked just like an old theatre should; the striking picture panel of the Spanish Armada

on the door. If I'd actually *met* her, I think I'd have turned into a jibbering, embarrassed, self-conscious heap – and what a terrible waste that would have been!

So, just imagine my childish excitement, when I learnt that my dancing school was planning to give a special performance of our annual pantomime in the Palace Theatre, and that I was actually going to be allowed to dance on the very stage where Beryl Grey had dazzled only a few months before. I had just three numbers: the sailor's dance that opened the second half, and two more appearances in the chorus as a villager.

While the first half of the pantomime jollied its way along, I went off to explore the cavernous dressing-rooms, and scenery stores down in the cellars under the stage. Wandering in that world of tarnished tinsel and fake trees, I lost all sense of time and direction, and eventually found myself climbing over the trap door mechanism right under the stage. Above I could hear dancers' feet thumping on the boards, and the faint strains of a tune I vaguely recognised. The sick feeling in the pit of my stomach told me that what I was hearing was my opening number. This was my big moment, and I'd missed my entrance. I ran all the way back up the stairs and stood panting and tearful in the wings watching the rest of the troupe perform without me. I changed into my next costume, determined not to be left behind again, and put on a brave face when my grinning companions asked with juvenile malice, 'What happened to you, then?' When you're ten, missing your entrance in the dancing school Show of the Year is like the end of the world, and try as I might, I couldn't get over my disappointment.

At the end of the show, proud mums and dutiful relatives came back-stage to hug and congratulate us like they do in the 'real' theatre. My mother thought I was marvellous – my aunt was more direct. 'I picked you out easily enough,' she said. 'You were the only kid there who didn't have a smile on her face – you looked miserable.' The flood gates opened, I wept buckets, and I think that was the moment I realised I wasn't cut out for a life on the stage!

THE CITY

The first, and only, newspaper I ever worked for as a reporter had its offices up in the roof of a four-storey building at the top of Royal Parade, Plymouth. The view from my desk, through long metal-framed windows, was not geared to inspire a budding young journalist! It offered a curious split image effect with the lower half blanked out by a concrete parapet some three foot high leaving only an empty sky and the flat roofs and square pigeon-hole offices of the other four-storey buildings opposite, to fill the top half of the picture. It wasn't until you walked out onto the flat roof behind the parapet, and looked down the length of the city's main thoroughfare that you could appreciate some of the vision that had inspired the planners and see why so many people label our modern city as being 'beautiful'.

Royal Parade is a tree-lined dual carriageway, flanked on one side by a block of creamy white Portland stone that tapers away for a quarter of a mile, housing shops and offices, department stores and banks. In the summer, the blank walls shimmer in the heat of the sun, giving a Mediterranean glare to the streets during the day and turning rose pink and orange in the garish glow of a multi-coloured sunset.

In contrast, the buildings on the left defy the straight lines and modular thinking of post-war planners, decorating the skyline with towers and turrets. St Andrew's Church must have one of the loveliest city settings in the country, surrounded as it is by an oasis of green lawns and quiet places. On warm days, the ground is peppered with shop and office workers eating their sandwiches, snatching an hour's ultraviolet after a morning of neon, and feeding the pigeons. I often sat on one of the benches eating a lunchtime snack of apples and cheese and, on one occasion, felt my neck being attacked by two of the city pigeons. Shades of Hitchcock? Not quite. I was wearing a necklace made out of dried seeds – and to the pigeons, they looked like a tasty meal!

St Andrew's Church was born with a natural grace in 1385 and six hundred years of architects won't better it. During the main wartime blitz on the city in March

1941, the church was reduced to a smouldering shell. Within days, a crudely-painted sign appeared over the main door bearing the one word 'Resurgam', 'I will rise again'. That slogan became something of a battle cry to the people of Plymouth who rebuilt their city – and their church – with care and love. I don't pretend to be a deeply religious person, but like many people I can enjoy the cool, quiet calm that prevails inside all church buildings. No one ever dashes about or shouts in church. The pace and volume are automatically toned down, and five minutes in that peaceful atmosphere can be a welcome relief from the pressures of life. In St Andrew's, there's the added visual bonus of John Piper's six glorious technicolor windows.

I was married in this church, and although the day outside was black with thunder clouds, and it hosed down with torrential rain, inside, those rainbow-coloured panes radiated golden sunlight shot with fire-red and sparkling blue, and no bride could ever have asked for a more beautiful day.

Behind St Andrew's, snuggled into the shelter of the east wall, is the Prysten House. In the fifteenth century, the priests and canons from Plympton Priory ran their ordered life on what was then the very edge of the old town, and in 1620 some of the Pilgrim Fathers are thought to have gathered for a prayer meeting under its timbered roof before sailing for a new life in America.

We can only guess at the horrors of that journey. One hundred and two souls were crammed onto the tiny

Royal Parade ; St Andrew's where I was married, and one of John Piper's magnificent windows ; the Prysten House

Mayflower which bucked and rolled across the Atlantic in storm-tossed seas for two and a half months. Not surprisingly, most of the Pilgrims were violently ill for much of the journey. Before they arrived, food and water had to be rationed, and when they finally sighted Cape Cod on 9 November 1620, one man had died and a son, Oceanus, had been born to Elizabeth Hopkins. To face such a journey, what they were running away from must have been horrific indeed!

Set into an outside wall of the Prysten House, there's yet another link with America, though perhaps a less honourable one.

A stone tablet records the names of two Americans, William Henry Allen, Commander of the U.S. ship *Argus*, and Midshipman Richard Delphey. Both died on 13 August 1813 following a sea battle in the English Channel against an English frigate and were buried in the churchyard of St Andrew's which lay between the church and the Prysten House. The headstone was presented to the city after the First World War by the National Society of the United States Daughters of 1812. Every year, on American Independence Day, civic dignitaries are joined by American representatives to honour those two long-ago casualties of war, and also the two hundred and eighty US soldiers and sailors who died in the apalling disease-ridden squalor of Dartmoor prison, fifteen miles away.

The gaol was originally built to house French prisoners of war who'd been rotting in six old hulks moored in Plymouth Sound. The fear of an epidemic spreading from the ships and sweeping through the town, persuaded the authorities to build a jail on the thirty-acre, god-forsaken bogs of Princetown, on the edge of Dartmoor Forest.

There are five two-storey rectangular blocks, built of granite and laid out like the spokes of a wheel inside a circle – each building could take up to fifteen hundred men and, in 1812, American prisoners started to join the French inside the prison. Two hundred and seventy-one of them died there, mostly from either typhoid or measles, but nine lost their lives in what the Americans call the Dartmoor Massacre.

Early in 1815, tempers reached flashpoint when four of their number emerged from one hundred days in the infamous punishment cell called the Cachot – a block house twenty feet square with just two openings at floor level, each six inches by four. There were no beds, no windows and no toilet facilities. Men had been known to die, or go mad after just a few weeks in this stone cage, but amazingly the four Americans survived, although their condition on their release in April 1815 shocked and angered the other prisoners into a state of near mutiny.

A few weeks later, peace was declared between America and England and, not unnaturally all the prisoners expected to be released, but a shortage of ships to carry them home meant that they had to stay in prison without any hope of leaving for some months. What had been smouldering animosity erupted into full-scale rebellion. The prisoners raided the food store, the guards charged with fixed bayonets, and three minutes later there were sixty-three casualties, and nine men dead. They were buried in the fields around the prison and, although during this century the Daughters of 1812 put up a memorial on the site of their official war graves at Princetown, it's at the Prysten House, near the appropriately named Door of Unity, that they're honoured and remembered each year.

Just ten paces away from that spot is a building I've always thought of as belonging to a Gilbert and Sullivan

The Guildhall – almost out of a Gilbert and Sullivan set

set. Plymouth's Guildhall was built in 1800 and has its corners softly rounded with turrets that are topped with inverted ice cream cones; a tower of medieval proportions, and window frames that look as if they were iced on in cement by some giant cake decorator, all of which helps to make it for me one of the most visually interesting and attractive buildings in the city. I covered my first 'Royal' story in that great hall, resplendent in Mother's best black wide-brimmed straw hat.

As Captain General of the Royal Marines, Prince Philip had come to the city to present new colours to the regiment and was later entertained to lunch in the Guildhall. The city 'plate' was out in force and sparkled with star-bursts of reflected light from the three crystal chandeliers. I sat at the end of one long trestle-table, eating my caterers' chicken, surrounded by city pomp and military glory, and couldn't believe my luck at being there. To crown my day, the editor gave me a by-line for my report. It was the first time I'd ever had a story acknowledged as 'by Angela Rippon', and I reckoned I'd arrived. I was still very much a junior reporter in the middle of serving the statutory three-year apprenticeship, but somehow it was like getting ten out of ten and a gold star for effort and I started to feel like a real reporter instead of just a 'cub'.

Ivybridge and Ermington

The *Sunday Independent*'s office was a strange one in which to work, for anyone who happened to blunder onto our floor unintentionally could easily have mistaken the row of anonymous doors along a windowless corridor and the incessant clatter of typewriters for just another insurance office. There was no rumble from the press, no smell of ink and boiling lead from the print machines, no urgent bustle to get the bundles of newsprint off the machines, into the vans and onto the street.

All that happened ten miles away in the village of Ivybridge. Because our main publication was a Sunday newspaper, half the staff would drive out to the print works to put the paper to bed on Saturday afternoons, leaving just a skeleton crew in the newsroom to make the regular round of calls to hospitals, ambulance, police

and fire stations – all of them good sources of information for a late-night story. As junior, that job always fell to me. So that, without my ever getting a smudge of printer's ink on my fingers, the finished paper would be thrust through my letterbox on Sunday morning.

I might never have got to see the printing press at all were it not for the fact that we also published a weekly paper every Friday for the country district around Ivybridge to the east of Plymouth. Almost every Tuesday morning for the best part of two years, I nosed my little car Debbie away from the city boundary out onto the A38 and headed for open country. Up Plympton St Maurice hill, through Smithaleigh and past Lee Mill, all by-passed now by the new draughts-

The building which once housed the printing press

man-straight dual carriageway: then, there was just a
single carriage road that had to dodge and weave its way
around the irregular contours of a dozen different farms.

The printing works stood on the edge of Ivybridge
village at the end of a narrow side street. Nowadays, the
building is smartly renovated in full view of the new
road, and houses a firm which makes sails for yachts.
When I first saw it almost twenty years ago, it was a
ramshackled bundle of granite that looked as though it
had slipped gently off the road and settled itself
comfortably beside the banks of the River Erme to enjoy
an early, peaceful retirement. My employers were hardly
press barons and spent only a little of what they did have
on maintaining the building which had character and
charm to spare, but apparently very little mortar to hold
it together.

The ground floor of the building was an engineer's
delight, but would have made a more ambitious young
reporter's heart sink. Immediately inside the door
loomed an enormous blackened flat-bed press – the sort
that makes guest appearances in old Hollywood
westerns whenever an 'old tyme' newspaper office is

*The River Erme scurrying alongside the road, and the little
bridge on the way to the pub*

featured. 'She's a beauty' was the verdict of the engineers. 'Used to sing on a Saturday night when she was going well. Could still print in an emergency – but we use that thing now.' 'That' was probably the most ancient of the modern rolling presses in use at that time. I was told it had a 'nasty habit of jamming just when you're all set for an early night home', and although it lived on to be virtually a museum piece, it never won the affection afforded to old 'flat-bed'.

Unless the press was actually rolling, this part of the building was always strangely quiet, especially in contrast to the Case Room on the left where the chatter of men and machines made it sound like a parrot house in stereo. Modern typesetting is done on clinical computers which pulsate electronically and produce pristine photographic prints or reams of data tape, from which the newspaper eventually emerges. Those old machines were dirty and smelly. The typeface was moulded out of liquid lead and the ink got into your veins. At the end of the day, you knew you'd created a newspaper – you took half of it home on your shirt cuffs!

The stairs to the first floor were narrow and Dickensian, the floor boards so far apart you could look down on the men below. When the paper was bought, some years after I'd joined, by the International Publishing Corporation, the whole place was thrown into confusion by the news that two representatives of the new owners would be paying the works a visit. These men were giants in Fleet Street – literally. They must have weighed over fourteen stone apiece. So the floors were hurriedly strengthened, just in case they took the quick way down – through the ceiling – to inspect the machines!

The editor sat in the corner of the reporters' room, chain-smoking his way through every edition, and checking each word of copy that went into his paper. When a story had been corrected and headlined, he stuffed it into a tin can, and dropped it through a hole in the floor to the print room below, on the end of a long piece of string. Fleet Street was never like this.

But there were compensations, in the people, the pace of life and the view which was lovely. Perfectly framed in the oblong window of the reporters' room was the rounded mass of Western Beacon, and the southernmost edge of Dartmoor. In summer, it turned heather-purple, in autumn bracken-gold, and most winters wore a cap of snow and frost.

The building may have had its shortcomings but its location was superb, right in the middle of open unspoiled countryside surrounded by green fields and dairy herds, with the moor just nudging towards the centre of the village. As someone who'd lived in a city all my life, this was the nearest I'd come to experiencing the countryside as a place to live and work in rather than to visit as an overawed spectator. And the ritual of enjoying the village pub lunch is something I look back on with the fondest of memories.

From the printing works, the road snaked south for a mile and a half to the village of Ermington. The pattern of the fields dictated the curve and bend of the road which turned left then right then right again around three sides of a square to skirt Yeolands Farm. With each bend, the low neat stone walls gradually change into thick bush and tree-topped hedges. The branches of beech and oak stretch and arch across the road in an attempt to reach the other side, blotting out the sky under a tunnel of leaves. Then the road takes a sudden

The rounded mass of Western Beacon; Ermington's crooked church spire, and our destination – The First and Last

kick to the left over a low-walled bridge, the sky bursts in, and there is the River Erme, chuckling and scurrying along the roadside, racing you to the pub.

Ermington's landmark is the church spire. A whimsical thing as crooked as a hawthorn staff, with a definite list to starboard. Some say ''Twas the Devil's work', others say ''Twas the brickie' who used more mortar between the bricks on one side than the other. Either way, the precarious-looking spire has stood solid for a century, and no one has any intention of straightening it.

The First and Last is a typical village 'local'. The bar is the centre of activity. No plush upholstery and flock wallpaper here, just plain cream walls shadowed by a decade of subtly applied nicotine. Along one wall there was a long trestle-table with an assortment of wooden chairs and the decor was completed by a warm fire, cold beer and Doris's pasties – especially Doris's pasties. They were, without doubt, the best I've ever eaten. Home-made every morning with a touch of culinary genius. So many pub pasties are overloaded with potatoes and soggy pastry to bulk them up, but not these. Meat and potatoes, onions and turnips were all in the right proportions, diced, seasoned with black pepper, then sealed in a short-crust pastry case. The first bite released the unmistakable aroma in a shot of steam – my mouth waters even now at the thought of it.

Men from the village (always men; hardly, if ever, the women) wandered in and out swopping gossip for pints in that wonderful Devon dialect that stretches the vowels and rearranges the English language with scant regard for grammar. The earthy sounds have the visitors giggling at its quaintness, but there's a strength and a melody to the dialect that I never tire of hearing.

To begin with, I was a 'furriner'. A newcomer, and welcome, but definitely 'under review'. By the end of the first year, I'd been accepted as a 'regular' so I played darts with the locals, dined regularly on pasties, drank half a pint of cream stout, and thought I was the bee's knees. El Vino's might be the in-place for Fleet Street. But as a fledgling reporter, I decided the First and Last would take a lot of beating!

Mount Edgcumbe

There used to be a tobacconist's shop in Union Street in Plymouth called Pengelly's. An old-fashioned shop that didn't believe in showing all its wares in the window: they were stacked on shelves inside. Instead, the centre-piece of their display window was a dolls' house-sized model of Mount Edgcumbe house made entirely from small, light brown cigars. The model fascinated me, and I couldn't walk past the shop without stopping to count the numerous windows, try to see inside one of the towers, and wish that I could be left alone to play 'house' with it for just one afternoon.

The real Mount Edgcumbe house stands in the centre of rolling parkland on a knuckle of land that juts out into Plymouth Sound on the Cornish side.

It was a place that I visited often with my parents on fine Sundays as a 'treat' and, by the time I was ten, I thought I knew every inch of its tangled woodland, mysterious gardens and coastal walks. In my twenties as a young newspaper reporter, I was genuinely thrilled to be sent to interview the new Earl and Countess, and in my thirties returned twice to capture the beauty of the parkland and gardens on film. I never tire of Mount Edgcumbe, and it remains one of my favourite places in England.

As a child, even the journey there was special, because it meant we had to travel across the water at the seaward end of the Tamar on the Cremyll Ferry.

The *Northern Belle* is a chunky little tub that has plied backwards and forwards across that narrow strip of water from Stonehouse to Cremyll beach for nearly fifty years. In 1945, they took out her steam engine and replaced it with diesel. But apart from that, she hasn't changed one jot in half a century. Shining brass, varnished seats and a regular coat of navy blue paint ensure that she wears her age well.

We would embark then, as people do now, at Admiral's Hard, an unlikely little mooring squeezed between the backyards of Stonehouse in a side road off Durnford Street. The tarmac of the road comes to an abrupt end in a mess of cobble and potholes, while the pavement strides out into the water to form the jetty.

The fare was 3d for adults, three halfpence for children – and that's something that *has* changed. The ten-minute journey now costs 25p, five shillings in 'real' money, but it's still worth it for the ride.

The *Belle* would bully her way across the clear bottle-green sea, dwarfed by the magnificent bulk of the Royal William Victualling Yard that's just around the corner from the tiny landing stage. If you didn't know its real purpose, you might almost think the 'Yard' was a misplaced Venetian winter palace with pillared façade and decorated cornices turned butter-yellow by the reflected rays of the sun. But it was the view ahead that always held my attention. A narrow pebble beach backed by a wall of black railings and, beyond, the gentle upward curve of tree-lined green lawns that marked the entrance to the park. Once the boat came alongside the Cremyll jetty, we would scramble up the sea-washed steps, pass through the old iron turnstile at the top, and make for the park gates.

Sir Richard Edgcumbe built the first house on this site in the mid-sixteenth century and, over the years, successive generations have improved the building, the gardens and parkland. None of the great architects or landscapers seems to have been involved in planning the estate. The Edgcumbes largely relied on their own judgment and good taste. And my word, they knew a thing or two about planning. It must have been marvellous to drive up the steady slope of parkland, in a carriage and pair, under the avenue of chestnut trees and watch the house grow ever more dominant on the sky line; then sweep away under the trees, over a small bridge and across the gravel drive to stop in front of the classic square Tudor house with its round turrets and granite mullioned windows. Oh, for the age of elegance!

My arrivals were less spectacular, we would walk across the grass to find a suitable picnic spot, and look up, not at a beautifully preserved manor house, but a fire-blackened, derelict shell. Mount Edgcumbe was gutted by incendiary bombs on the night of 22 April

Mount Edgcumbe House and the colourful French garden

1941, and it was seventeen years before work began on rebuilding that lovely old house.

Although the park was always open to the public, the house and its immediate gardens were strictly out of bounds, a situation that made them highly desirable places in which to be. So the scanty, rusting barbed wire fence was more of a challenge than a deterrent. It was so easy to slip undetected through the brambles and under the wire, and the fact that I knew I shouldn't be there made it by far the most interesting part of the estate. On one visit I found a huge fir cone from the old tree which still dominates one corner of the lawns. The size of a healthy pineapple, my father later varnished it and made it into a bedside lamp for me.

I was eventually cured of my clandestine visits when one Sunday afternoon I emerged from the tangle of undergrowth and barbed wire to see a tall, slim figure in a straw hat standing by the west door. It was old Lady Mount Edgcumbe herself. I fled in panic before she saw me, and never went back again – uninvited.

Which is why I couldn't believe my luck when I was sent by the *Sunday Independent* more than ten years later to interview the new Earl and Countess of Mount Edgcumbe who inherited the title in 1965. The Earl was always referred to by his wife as 'Edgy' – a name used endearingly now by many people when speaking of him, and what a darling old man he is. We dubbed him 'The Reluctant Earl' after the interview, as in many ways that's exactly what he is.

Having spent a lifetime in New Zealand as a wealthy sheep farmer, he suddenly found himself the last living member of the family to bear the name of Edgcumbe, as the previous earl's only son and heir had been killed at Dunkirk. Edgy came to Cornwall, took up the trappings of nobility, but regretted not being able to join the men working on the estate. 'They won't let me,' he would say. 'They tell me it's not fitting for the Earl.' So he compromised; for official functions, he's happy to turn up in his best bib and tucker, but at home he works comfortably in ancient grey flannels tied at the waist with an old leather belt, a collarless shirt, a straw hat of dubious origins, and shoes that have seen more muck heaps than polish. Dressed in this fashion, he works on the flower beds and lawns surrounding the house. He is genuinely delighted when people mistake him for the gardener and won't ever let on that he's really the Earl.

Over the years, I've come to know him and like him enormously, but it was one of those wicked bits of deception that completely took me in at our first meeting. I'd never seen either the new Earl nor his wife when I arrived at the house with a photographer to interview them for the newspaper. We went to the front door, known as the Royal Entrance, rang the bell, and had the double oak doors opened to us by a grey-haired gentleman in tweeds. 'I'm here to interview the Earl for the *Sunday Independent*,' I said. 'We are both expected.'

'Yes, of course,' said the man, whom I naturally took to be the butler, 'please come this way.'

He showed us into the lovely domed hall at the centre of the house, took our coats, opened the door on the drawing-room and, offering us a seat, said 'Her Ladyship will be down in a minute.'

Her Ladyship duly arrived a few moments later, offered us tea, and said her husband would join us shortly. We were both well into a conversation about her charitable work in New Zealand when the door opened and in came the butler. Her Ladyship stood up, held out her hand, and announced, 'Ah, here's my husband – the Earl.' He grinned like a small boy who'd beaten everyone at charades, and won me over completely.

The estate is really divided into three sections, the house, the formal gardens, which are some way from the main building on the water's edge, and the parkland – all 865 acres of it stretching from the Cremyll Ferry around the coast for ten miles to the rugged cliffs of Rame Head. In my teens, I often walked along the track of The Earl's Drive – parts of which are now incorporated into the coastal footpath – to the halfway point of that ten-mile walk, the twin villages of Cawsand and Kingsand. When the gorse is in bloom, the acid yellow flowers light up the

The twin villages of Cawsand and Kingsand

clifftop with bursts of unbelievable brightness, and as you emerge from the dark canopy of trees on the wooded hillside, out into the first large clearing beyond Fort Picklecombe, the bright rays of an August sun can turn the whole of Cawsand Bay into a garish canvas of colour. No subtle hues of the water-colourist here, but startling yellow sharp against dark green foliage, sun-bleached rocks fringed with the nodding heads of pink thrift and red valerian, stately heads of rose bay willowherb jostling each other for the breeze, and the sea a crystal clear blue that would shame the Mediterranean.

When the tramp across the cliffs was just too far, I'd make instead for the Ruin. It looks like the remains of a small Gothic church, but in fact it's nothing more than a folly, built as a ruin to look picturesque on the hillside – a job it does beautifully. And when you stand on the slopes around the ruin to look out at the view, you can understand why the earls of the eighteenth century chose this spot as a focal point for visitors on their walks through the woods.

The Ruin, a picturesque folly ; Millbrook (left) and Plymouth seen from Mount Edgcumbe's extensive parkland

Drake's Island floats in the middle of an expanse of sparkling water, which itself is hemmed in by the roofs of Plymouth, the green fields of Devon farms and, beyond, the soft rolling purple hills of Dartmoor.

It's a haven for birds up here too, especially green woodpeckers who thrive on the millions of insects living in the dead trees which have been left to create perfect woodpecker habitat.

The parkland has been open to the general public for years. Only during the last war did it become a restricted area while American tanks and troop landing craft trundled under the boughs and past the daffodil banks, well camouflaged from prying eyes during their preparations for the D Day landings. When the park was re-opened, picnickers and walkers found a legacy of concrete roads laced through the woods, making the whole area far more accessible than it had ever been.

But there was still one section of the estate that remained something of a tangled mess and attracted little, if any, attention. The formal gardens are almost a quarter of a mile away from the house at the bottom of the drive with the sea forming a boundary on two sides; a high stone wall and an iron fence completing the square.

Originally, the formal gardens had been laid out as a 'divertissement' for visitors to the house. A patchwork of Italian, French and English gardens, separated by tall hedges and linked by neat paths. Somewhere to amble through on a warm spring day, or summer's morning, to take in the fabulous kaleidoscope of colour from flowers and shrubs, the cool gentle splash of water from elegant fountains, and the shade of exotic canopied trees. Well – that's what it *was* like. But after the war, those who ventured under the stone-arched entrance found moss-riddled lawns, a jungle of undergrowth and only the merest shadow of a former beauty.

In 1971, the parkland was bought by Plymouth City and Cornwall County Councils, and the gardeners who moved in were given the opportunity of a lifetime – to re-create, as accurately as possible, the elegance and glory of those eighteenth-century gardens. I visited the estate often and made two films there with the head gardener, Dick Wood, a well-rounded, ruddy-cheeked man of the soil, who grew more and more excited as 'his' garden emerged from a choking blanket of weeds, to reveal precision-planned flower beds, low box hedges, forgotten rose gardens and a pattern of paths that curved and meandered through the plants, surprising the eye with yet more beauty at every twist and bend.

The Italian garden, as you might expect, has a dominant staircase topped with balustrades and classical statues which look down on a central fountain, and the clean, oblong lines of an orangery. During summers of the early nineteenth century, the orange trees would be brought out of their glass-fronted hot-house and lined up with regimental neatness around the edges of the lawns. Each diminutive tree in its own wooden barrel, with the orange fruits glowing on a bed of rich dark leaves. It must have looked magnificent. The fruit trees are long since gone, replaced inside the orangery by a cafeteria, and outside by beds of spring wallflowers and summer annuals.

A tall box hedge and gentle stroll along a path at the bottom of a sloping lawn separate the Italian from the French garden – the favourite spot of the first Countess of Mount Edgcumbe, Sophia, who lived there around the turn of the nineteenth century. It's said that she would sit for hours in the sunny seclusion of this garden, hemmed in by tall evergreen hedges, with the flower beds bordered by tiny privet hedges, and filled with colourful blooms to create the impression of a Persian carpet while, in the centre, the fountain splashed water into a huge clam shell. Just sitting there for a few moments, with the gentle sound of water, and of bees busily droning about their business, it's not difficult to see why Sophia, and so many people since, have found this corner of the gardens so restful.

In direct contrast, the garden next door that is labelled 'English', doesn't have a flower bed in sight. Just an acre of sweeping lawn, shaded by large, elderly specimen trees from all over the world. There are the waxy blooms of the magnolia, the gnarled irregular features of the Spanish cork tree, the strange fan-shaped leaves of the ginkgo, or maidenhair tree, and the delicate white fronds that give *Davidia involucrata* its more graphic and common name of the handkerchief tree. I couldn't understand why a garden so full of foreigners should be called 'English' and was told by Dick Wood, 'It's not the content that gives the name – but the style.'

Just below the 'English' lawns is a small dell that you might almost pass by without even noticing. Dick and his men have always called it the Fernery, and certainly the shady cool hollow is a perfect place for growing ferns

The Italian garden with its classical statues

and those plants that like the darker, damper parts of a garden. Sticking up between the almost transparent fronds are a number of large boulders, and a collection of small headstones, each one bearing the name of a much loved family pet. This is where the Mount Edgcumbes buried their dogs. No doubt, the animals appreciated the cool of this place when they were alive, so it's an appropriate place for them to snooze out eternity.

I remember coming out of the Fernery on my first visit there, and finding that I'd walked through an archway cut into an evergreen oak hedge of truly monumental proportions. It stretched up for over thirty feet, and was more than fifty yards long. These days, one man can trim the hedge into straight geometric lines in a few hours using an electric trimmer. But before mechanical cutters were invented, the hedge was trimmed by a gang of some two dozen men, who worked over every inch of that mass of greenery for more than a week, coaxing it into shape with hand-pruners. It doesn't bear thinking about!

In 1976, the International Camelia Society planted two hundred camelias in the garden, creating what has become one of the most glorious spectacles in the county every spring when the trumpets of pink and cream flowers are in full bloom. I was walking through the gardens not long after that mammoth tree-planting exercise, and found Dick Wood and his men clearing yet another wall of brambles and weeds, and planting in the newly tilled clearing, hundreds of small azalea trees. When I left, a few hours later, Dick presented me with two soggy, lumpy newspaper parcels, each containing an azalea 'seedling' no more than eight inches high. 'I know how much you love this place,' he said, 'and thought you'd like to take a bit of it home with you.' I could have cried.

The small trees have done well on the slopes of my Dartmoor garden. They're now almost two feet high. And every spring when the golden yellow buds start to swell and fatten in the pale moorland sunshine, I feel a little closer to that other 'favourite' garden in Cornwall, fifteen miles away on the slopes of the River Tamar.

The South Hams

You won't find the South Hams named as such on any map I know of. But they exist – you can be sure of that. The Hams are those small villages and hamlets that fill the southern pockets of Devon, hemmed in by the Rivers Erme and Dart, with their northern boundary the main road from Totnes to Ivybridge, their southern limit, the sea. There are signposts on the roads which say 'Welcome to the South Hams', as if you were entering a specific geographical area like a county or a town, whereas what they're really welcoming you to is another world, where the pace of life is set by the seasons, and where the leafy lanes, the patchwork of fields, and rural communities have largely avoided the attentions of twentieth-century modernisation.

Around its coastline, there are some of the finest beaches in the county, and tucked away behind high hedges and under thatched roofs are some of the friendliest country pubs in which you could ever wish to relax. It was an area I came to know and love in the mid 1950s when, perched on my bicycle and following the familiar outline of my father, we pedalled away my juvenile summers.

Because my mother was out to work for five days a week, Saturdays were family days when we shopped or went to the cinema together. But Sunday was her day for catching up on the household chores so she would willingly pack off my father and me with sandwiches and cake to explore the countryside, while she got on with the dusting and ironing.

As for my father, he didn't seem to mind spending most Sundays in the company of his seven-year-old daughter. He'd been at sea until I was three, and in all that time saw me on only one brief visit home. So he had missed out on the years when I'd progressed from crawling in nappies and mumbling gibberish, to walking and talking. He told me once, 'I felt I had a lot of lost time to make up,' which is presumably why he filled those Sundays with so much discovery and fun, telling me about his own boyhood in County Durham, and

A patchwork of fields and hedges in the South Hams

passing on his own pleasure in the countryside about us.

The lanes of the South Hams are hedge-lined and tree-shaded. Few people could afford the luxury of cars in those days, so most of our fellow travellers were either like us, on two wheels, or walking, taking life at a leisurely pace which left time to examine the beauty of a hedgerow and listen to bird song.

But if the pace of life is easy in the South Hams, the hills are not. As in most of Devon, they plummet down, often twisting around blind corners and fiendish zig-zags, then lure you up deceptively steep gradients where wooded hillsides and gentle valley views help to take your mind off your pounding heart and aching legs. Uphill, my skinny muscles found the going hard. That's when Father would ride beside me with one hand on the back of my saddle, pushing me up the hill, while his own service-hardened muscles pedalled furiously. Downhill, he'd ride ahead, to make sure that I didn't go hurtling at breakneck speed to the bottom. Once my courage failed, and I jammed on the brakes. The front wheel skidded, and I somersaulted over the handlebars. There was a lot of blood and a few scratches, but the impact hadn't altered the shape of my face too much, so we pressed on to the beach at Bigbury.

All the beaches along that coastline boast miles of golden sand, clear water and stunning cliff-top scenery. Bigbury has the added attraction of an offshore island that's accessible at low tide; also a collection of shops and cafés that dispense candy floss, ice cream and endless cups of tea.

A few years ago, I had cause to be grateful for the tea, not to mention a gallon of warming soup and an endless supply of steaming hot dogs. I was the editor of a women's programme for Westward, the local ITV station, and took a group of model girls with a film crew to the beach at Bigbury to make a film about a new collection of swimwear. It was an ideal location, with the sea, the island and the beach as a backdrop. Only we

made the film in March when the temperature was barely human, and the knife-edge on the wind turned the girls into bikini-clad lumps of shivering, blue gooseflesh. Only the comfort of woollen blankets, and endless cups of warming soup and coffee prevented a mutiny, and got the film finished.

It was also at Bigbury that I was able to watch two young thatchers at work on the roof of one of the cottages in the village. Gayling Greenwell and his younger brother Terry were both in their early twenties. They'd recently completed a three-year apprenticeship with the Rural Industries Training Board to learn the skills of a craft that had suffered something of a depression in South Devon as the decorative, but

A sunny ramble down a typical Devon lane; Bigbury beach and one of the village's thatched cottages

expensive thatch had been overtaken by tiles and roof slates.

Using reeds grown in mid-Devon at Winkleigh and Ashreighney, and tools similar to those that had been wielded by craftsmen for generations, the two young men worked in quiet harmony, pinning each bundle of reeds in place with a hooped spar of willow or hazel, and cropping them to shape with a spar hook – a sort of curved machete.

While they worked, I interviewed them perched on a ladder forty feet up, with my elbows in the gutter trying to look comfortable – though I wasn't – and as if it was quite normal for me to conduct interviews balanced on people's roofs. On film, it looked most impressive, and the programme editor was delighted when a viewer wrote to say that if he was going to make a habit of sending lady reporters to interview people whilst draped decorously up ladders, he'd watch our programme for ever in favour of the opposition on the other channel!

A few miles along the coast from Bigbury is my favourite of the South Hams beaches – Thurlestone. The village is one of those chocolate-box communities of pink-washed thatched cottages with roses round the doors. It's a genteel place where retired colonels and Knightsbridge weekenders can enjoy a *Homes and Gardens* rural existence.

You have to drive through the village to reach Thurlestone beach which is a perfect crescent of soft sand backed by gentle rolling farmland and overlooked from one end by a superb cliff-top golf course. There are no ice cream kiosks, cafés or commercialisation of any description, just half a mile of unspoiled beach dominated by the Thurlestone Rock – a hoop of stone that was once joined to the land, but now stands a few yards offshore, in splendid isolation, like a triumphant arch that's gone for a paddle in the briny.

I've lain on that beach, scorched by the sun of July and August, watching the sails of small craft bob crimson and white against the sea, and echoed the thoughts of so many of my countrymen. 'If only we could guarantee the weather, who would ever want to go abroad for their holidays?'

The beach is so close to Plymouth that once when I had a car of my own, I would often dash out of the city after work to snatch a few hours of late sun before the shadows lengthened and turned into dusk.

Thurlestone Rock, with the lovely sandy beach

Hallsands and Beesands

It's very easy to spend a lifetime in an area and still not know every nook and cranny, so I was not really surprised when my husband Christopher plonked his finger on the map, obliterating the name 'Hallsands' and declared, 'I've never been there.'

I had. Just once, to interview one of the community's few surviving former inhabitants – Mrs Evelyn Lamble. I wasn't the first reporter to turn up on her doorstep to ask for her story – nor the last. In fifty years, a whole string of journalists had come in search of Mrs Lamble and her neighbours to hear how, on the night of 26 January 1917, the sea had finally lost patience with the clutch of houses on the edge of its territory, and smashed them into oblivion.

The Hallsands of Mrs Lamble's childhood had been a busy, self-contained fishing village in which nearly two hundred souls lived and worked in unison. The houses were built at the bottom of a steep cliff, their foundations perched precariously on a shelf of natural rock and concrete. They had a post office and pub – The London Inn – a seamen's mission and general shop. There were

'The Old Village' – Hallsands has been deserted since it was destroyed by ferocious storms in 1917

also stables for the pack horses that carried loads up and down the steep track cut into the side of the hill which was the only way in or out of the village by land. A narrow lane ran the length of the village – all 200 yards of it – flanked by houses which had their backs to the cliffs on one side, and their faces to the full blast of the south-westerlies on the other. A bank of shingle some ninety feet wide absorbed the full force of winter gales and allowed the fishermen of Hallsands to rest safely within touching distance of the petulant, unpredictable sea.

In 1896, the shingle bar was raided by engineers from Plymouth who wanted the fine smooth pebbles to make concrete for the extensions to Devonport Dockyard. No one minded. The sea had, after all, built the shingle bar unaided, and the men of Hallsands were confident that Neptune would repair the damage done by man. But he didn't and the erosion continued – until that night in 1917 when the combination of a very high tide and gale force winds smashed through all that remained of the flimsy defences and started ripping the houses apart. For four days the storm raged, unabated. No lives were lost but walls collapsed, foundations were sucked out and at the end of it, 'the sea was full of furniture'. Mrs Lamble never tired of telling her story, and recited it without dramatic overtones or embellishments, but in a direct almost detached narrative that somehow made it more poignant. She had witnessed and been part of something that I, fifty years later, could only attempt to conjure up in my mind's eye, and I knew that the comfortable surburban life I'd lived, away from the whims of the elements and the horrors of natural disasters, found me lacking.

Mrs Lamble told of how families huddled together in corners watching the waves snatch at their homes, crashing violently over their heads through the long black nights. Of how the wind 'roared like thunder as if the world was coming to an end' and how she prayed and prayed for the storm to abate.

One by one, the surviving families, including Mrs Lamble, found other homes further along the coast and in the next small bay called New Hallsands. Only Miss Elizabeth Prettijohn remained. Her family lived in the one house that escaped any damage since it was built just out of reach, a little higher up the hill than the rest. She lived on in the small family home – the self-appointed guide and historian of the village.

People who met her found that energy and sparkle belied her sixty-plus years. Each day she would stride out across the cliffs to the next village to help the fishermen with their catch, and she walked most days to the farm on the hill for milk. Her home was shared by a few chickens and a lot of ghosts and, when she died, the last breath of life finally went out of Hallsands village.

Since meeting Mrs Lamble, I'd never been back to the drowned village so Christopher's curiosity was a good excuse to renew my acquaintance. It was New Year's Eve – a day when the rest of Britain shivered under plummetting temperatures and gale force winds while, in the south-west, we enjoyed one of those God-given days when the sky is clear ice blue, the wind settled and the world lit by soft sunshine.

Our route took us through Kingsbridge, through West and East Charleton, the thatched quaintness of Frogmore, and into Chillington where a signpost indicated right to the village of Hallsands and its neighbour Beesands. The road unfolded in a series of gentle hills that pitched and rose into the distance like a huge roller-coaster. At the summit of each hill, we were faced with another fold of neat, empty green fields, then another and another, each hill tantalisingly obscuring the sea. Christopher's question 'Are you sure we're on the right road?' was immediately answered at a cross-roads by a multi-armed signpost which pointed un-erringly onward to the summit of another horizon. At the top, the main road disappeared on into the distance, but the Hallsands sign took us sharp left and downhill onto an unlikely-looking single track. Ahead, sea and sky were so blue, they merged into one with only the slim dark finger of the Dartmouth headland fifteen miles away to mark the dividing line.

We parked the car and walked the last hundred yards or so to the cliff edge where the ground rises gently so it's

impossible to see down onto the beach until you're virtually on the brink. A small wooden sign at the top of the well-worn track indicated 'The Old Village' as if it knew exactly what we'd come looking for, and as we turned down to walk across the cliff face, there was the village, or what's left of it, at our feet.

Miss Prettijohn's cottage was still intact. Boarded up now, waiting patiently for its summer visitors. And the rest was just as I had remembered – a shingle cove traversed by flat-topped rocks and the weird, almost surrealist outline of a single end wall standing defiantly intact, its fireplace and windows staring blindly out to sea.

The face of the cliff still holds on protectively to a few back walls and chimney stacks of some of the rear cottages. The wooden lintels are intact, the rusting drainpipes play tunes in the wind and a back door stands ever open. Apart from the rocks, the beach is littered with huge slabs of concrete that once bolstered the foundations of the buildings and provided a low sea wall. We clambered over them and the rocks to reach the one building that stands with four walls, almost intact.

There are warning signs: 'These buildings are dangerous', which they undoubtedly are, but if you're intrigued by history, always searching for some colour from the past, who can resist them?

We traced with ease the foundations of an old piggery and could see clearly where the little street had laced through the houses. In a pile of rubble, Chris found a small square of broken china, striped brown and orange on white and crazed into a million fine veins. The remains of a fisherman's mug perhaps, a family tea-service smashed by the storm, or just the debris from a broken cup left by more recent picnickers? Who can say. But it was the only splash of colour in an otherwise drab and crumpled world.

I stood in the front door of the house looking out at the English Channel, the cliff face brooding behind me, the sea gently rustling the shingle not three feet away and thought, 'They must have been mad to live here.' Hallsands' fishermen, more than any of their colleagues along that coastline, were truly part of the sea, living on its boundary, allowing it to lap against their lives, and although the sea finally threw them out, I have to admit you must admire their tenacity for trying.

As we walked back up the hill away from the ruins, the whole sweep of Start Bay was strung out in front of us. 'What's over there?' asked Chris, pointing north to a narrow strip of sunlit beach. 'Beesands,' I said. 'I suppose you haven't been there either.' He shook his head. 'We can either drive round, or walk along the coastal footpath – which do you fancy?' We both took in the flat calm of the sea, the unexpected warmth of the sun, and decided the day was too good to waste stuck in a car – so headed for the footpath.

Before we'd gone fifty paces, we had to take a detour. It isn't only Hallsands that has succumbed to the fury of the sea along this coast. Every year, the contours are changed as yet another bit of clifftop surrenders to the persistent action of the waves and, not two miles away, the seaward end of the village of Torcross has been gradually chipped away, without the sudden drama of Hallsands, but all of its misery. We could see the line the coastal path used to take, worn down to smooth earth through tough grasses and brambles. It slipped under a rusty barbed wire barricade, then came to a jagged precipitous end where a wedge of land had broken away, flinging the path, and a huge chunk of field, sixty feet down onto the beach.

The short detour took us around the back of what no doubt had once been a lovely stone house. The windows looked out over the gracious curve of the bay and inland to the green fields and estuaries of south Devon. But seagulls wheeled where the garden had been, and the front wall was only a few feet from the cliff edge. It had been left, a burnt-out shell, its fate inevitable. A few paces away, the path dropped down towards the cliff edge in front of a row of terraced cottages, the 'For Sale' sign in one window no doubt put there in hope rather than expectation. For although the buildings look sound enough, and the path is intact, the skinny naked stalks that were last year's brussel sprouts are a give-away. They stand erect in front of the buildings, but lurch

drunkenly a few feet on and disappear completely before the end of the row.

Ironically, these were the cottages that housed some of the families who'd fled from Hallsands in 1917. Defeated at sea level, they must have believed they'd be safe perched on the cliffs, high above the waves. Sixty-three years later, their descendants know better! We walked past the cottages, down the hill towards the pebble beach of New Hallsands. There was a hopeless dereliction about the buildings, and I wasn't sad to leave them behind. A few fishermen stood expectantly beside rods anchored in the ground, lines trailing out into water. Their baskets were empty, but the sun was warm, the beach virtually deserted. It was a good way to spend the day.

At the far end of the beach, the ground rose up in a sudden, sharp hill, taking the path back onto the cliff. We started climbing, moving higher and higher and, like a pair of human helicopters, watching the shore recede below us. All along this stretch of coastline, the fields run down to the very edge of the land, separated from sea and shingle by just our thin highway of mud – and a sixty-foot drop. For those who care about such things, it provides a wonderful contrast of habitat and wildlife as farmland and seashore rub shoulders. Thrift and sea campion bloom within yards of pennywort and foxgloves, with finches and robins plucking worms and seeds from recently ploughed fields, while guillemots and oystercatchers seek their own harvest on the seaward side of the boundary.

Ahead the path began a gentle descent to the village of Beesands and the strip of beach that seemed to stretch forever from Limpet Rocks to Slapton, and Pilchard Cove glowed golden in the last fierce rays of the afternoon sun. Smoke trailed lazily from the cottage chimneys, a pile of lobster pots looked dry and salty as though unused for months, and one old man stood outside his home, chopping logs with careful aim and measured strokes. Perhaps Hallsands had once looked like this, the rows of cottages neat and cared for, the shore lined with small boats and nets, all evidence of a working community, and it was charming.

We decided to walk back to our car along the shoreline and ducked under the lines of two more fishermen – mirror images of their counterparts a mile away at the other end of the beach.

'Caught anything?'

'No. Not a bite all day. Maybe we'll have done better when you come back.' Only we didn't intend to come back – not that day, at least.

The sun was now so low in the sky that the cliffs threw a deep shadow along the shore, slicing it in two. Out of the sun, it was chilly and dull, so we walked along the water's edge, soaking up the last, warm rays of that exceptional winter's day. The beach, that had looked like sand from the top of the cliffs, turned out to be made of small shingle pebbles and, in our wellingtons, it was a bit like walking on ball-bearings. Agony on the leg muscles – so it must have been doing us good.

Salt-washed and gleaming in the light, the stones were irresistible and we both found ourselves, first bent, then crouched over a promising looking patch, searching intently for pebbles that were brighter, more unusually coloured or shaped than the next. The combination of various rocks in the area, from sandstone to granite, has produced a mixture of rare colour and beauty that ranges from translucent cream and pink, to pale brown, deep burgundy, through slate grey and black. No wonder, as children, we collected pebbles for 'jewels' – but what a disappointment to get them home and find that, away from the sea, they'd dried to a dull matt blob.

Chris found a black hot cross bun, then a heart. My find was a piece of sandstone quite definitely shaped like a C; there had to be an A somewhere to go with it – but we didn't find it. For a mile, we walked in and out of the surf, back towards Hallsands, shooting flat pebbles across the waves like dambusters, and revelling in the unique sensation of having an entire beach to ourselves, for even the statuesque cormorants, who'd perched on the rocks like figures cast in wrought iron, had retired to the sea. In the summer, it would be alive with children and sizzling bodies, but New Year's Eve was a day for log fires and turkey sandwiches, so we savoured our solitude and regretted not having brought the dogs. 'They'd have loved it,' said Chris, and we knew that was a good excuse for coming back.

A few evocative remains of Hallsands village; pebbles, salt-washed and gleaming in the sunlight

A Unique Nature Reserve

The road from Kingsbridge to Dartmouth twists and curves at a gentle pace through wooded hills and green fields, slipping through the villages and meandering with scant regard for straight lines or speed. But at the outskirts of Torcross, it changes character completely, leaving the woods and farmland behind. It strides out in a straight fast carriageway for two and a half miles right through the middle of a superb Devon nature reserve – Slapton Ley. On the right-hand side of the road, the sea crashes in from Start Bay onto a narrow shingle beach. In total contrast, on the left, there are the still calm waters of the Ley, a fresh-water lake fed by three small streams that tumble off the Devon hills to flood and feed the Ley like a bath with the taps constantly running. Only the shingle ridge, on which the road is built, prevents the sea from swamping the lake and that's what provides the county with a unique centre of wildlife.

Whenever I have to drive to Dartmouth, I always try to take that slower, winding route, rather than the quicker alternatives inland, and to add at least ten or fifteen minutes to my travelling time so that I can pull up at one of the parking spots along the road, and have a few minutes to myself. I'm not a bird-watching 'twitcher' – one of those enthusiasts who dart around the country-side marking off bird sightings like items in a catalogue. Admittedly, I enjoy spotting a rarity, like anyone else, but I get my pleasure in wild things from just watching and observing rather than collecting. There's such beauty in the pattern and iridescence of plumage, the antics of courtship, the skill of the hunter, that I'm always happy to surrender a few minutes of every day to the enjoyment of quiet observation. And at Slapton Ley, I've never yet been disappointed, or found my time empty and wasted.

Coot and mallard are familiar outlines on the water, as are the graceful lines of several pairs of swans. A large, dead oak tree on the land side of the lake has turned ghostly-white from the droppings of cormorants who have requisitioned the tree as a roost, and it's not

Slapton Ley, with soft rolling Devon farmland beyond

unusual to see anything up to thirty of those large black birds doing a balancing act on the branches.

Devon has so few freshwater lakes that the eighty-five hectares at Slapton are a haven for a whole list of spring and autumn migrants like the terns and widgeon, pochard and golden eye, although the most important annual visitor is undoubtedly the great crested grebe which was almost wiped out by the fashion trade of the nineteenth century which thought the birds' brilliant plumage would look better on ladies' hats than on the birds themselves. They disappeared from Devon in 1890, but a single pair returned in 1972, and several have bred successfully on the Ley ever since.

The water is very shallow. It's no more than three metres deep anywhere, and the rich mud silt on the bed is a veritable larder of food for pike, roach and perch as well as the thousands of birds who fly in and out each year. But during the summer, it's the visitors who provide a regular, alternative source of food, which is why Slapton is one of the few places in Britain to have a road traffic sign warning motorists to beware of ducks as they venture out of the water and across the road in search of tourists, and tasty tit bits!

It would be so easy for the Ley to look artificial and man-made with the tarmac road lying conveniently like a dam along one side. It isn't, of course. Nature arranged the land in this orderly fashion all by herself, and even though man came along a few thousand years later to make use of her ingenuity by adding a flat, featureless tarmac road, Nature replied by softening the stark lines with a fringe of tall, willowy reeds which border the lake and provide food and shelter for colonies of water rails and moorhens. In the summer, the marshes echo to the strident calls of warblers and reed buntings, and the frondy grasses provide camouflage for the statuesque form of that master fisherman – the heron.

The beach at Slapton is one of the few I know that boasts a crop of wild summer flowers, and there are no sights more attractive than the yellow heads of the horn

The rich mud silt provides food for both fish and birds

poppy scattered like freckles on the shoreline between rows of browning bodies. And just once, I was able to stand entranced with a whole beach full of people as a lone porpoise played in the waves a few yards from the land. It was a magical moment that's never been repeated – not for me at least.

In the 1950s, Slapton Ley became an official Nature Reserve, administered by the Field Studies Council. Over the years it has developed, not just as a haven and refuge for wildlife, but also as an important centre for research, education and recreation. The headquarters of the trust are in Slapton village itself, and all along the

Ley, there's evidence of its work, from the sign posts and information boards at the start of the Nature Trail to the protected areas of shingle fenced off from the public to allow a few delicate and rare plants to grow undisturbed.

It's such a natural, unspoiled part of the coastline that the great obelisk of granite halfway along the road sticks out, quite literally, like a sore thumb, but this is no war memorial for the dead; it's a symbol of thanks to the living, from the United States Army.

In 1943, the beach at Slapton was offered to the American forces of 'Operation Overlord' as a practice area for their D Day assault on Normandy the following summer. A triangle of land with Blackawton at its northern point, Strete and Torcross to the east and west, was emptied of all living things so that the forces could practise with live ammunition, in total secrecy. Everything was moved, the animals and crops were taken from the fields of one hundred and eighty farms, seven hundred and fifty families had to desert their homes, leaving everything to the mercy of the 'friendly' invaders. It was a monumental task, and even though the villagers harboured a certain pride in the knowledge that they were making a supreme contribution to the war effort, there was also sadness, tinged with despair and anxiety.

For more than six months, nearly three thousand souls were given temporary accommodation outside the area, some as far away as Scotland – never knowing what was happening inside the Security Zone. Each church in the seven parishes had a notice from the Bishop of Exeter pinned to the door. It read: 'TO ALL OUR ALLIES OF THE USA. This church has stood here for several hundred years, around it has grown a community which has lived in these houses and tilled these fields ever since there was a church. This church, this churchyard in which their loved ones lie at rest, their homes, these fields, are as dear to those who have left them as are the homes and granges and fields which you, our allies, have left behind you. They hope to return one day as you hope to return to yours to find them waiting to welcome them home. They entrust them to your care meanwhile, and pray that God's blessing may rest upon us all. Charles. Bishop of Exeter.'

The sentiments were clear, but the demands of war made them almost impossible to fulfil.

In the autumn of 1944, after the rehearsals at Slapton had been played out in full on the beaches of Normandy, families gradually started to move back into their homes. They cut down the bramble and thistle that had invaded their land, repaired the damage to fields and

The US Army's memorial, and a fine long-distance view of this unique nature reserve

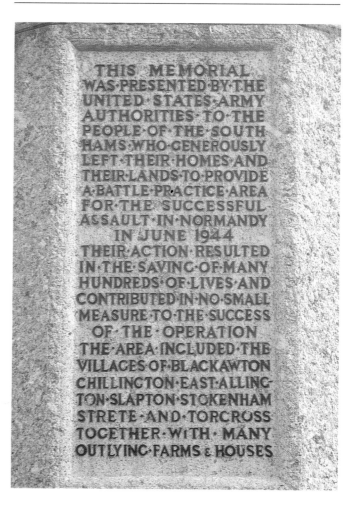

homes that were pitted and scarred from the bullets and bombs, and demolished those buildings that were beyond repair.

It took time to heal the scars, on both the land and in people's minds, although to look at the area now, it's difficult to realise that the war had such a devastating impact on this peaceful community. To sit, as I have done, quite still and quiet near the water's edge, waiting for the shy families of coot to float out from the protection of the reeds, listening to the spring chorus of bird song, and praying for a rare glimpse of the wary otters who find sanctuary in this lovely place, it's difficult to imagine the scene when the bay was crowded with ships and landing craft, the woods alive with bodies of camouflaged troops, and the valley ringing to the cacophony of war. But they were here, and the monument remains as a permanent 'thank you' to the people of Blackawton and Chillington, East Allington and Slapton, Stokenham, Strete and Torcross.

Blackpool Sands doesn't look a bit like its namesake on the Lancashire coast. If anything, this sheltered and very lovely bay, just round the corner from Slapton Ley, is more reminiscent of the Mediterranean – especially when the sun is shining.

Dartmouth and the Dart Valley

It's impossible to visit the town of Dartmouth and ignore the great red brick bulk of the Royal Naval College built in the first years of the twentieth century on Mount Boone above the town. If you approach by sea, through the narrow neck of land that almost disguises the harbour entrance, and pass under the gun turrets of Dartmouth Castle, the college sits four-square and solid, dead ahead. While from the streets of the town, and the pavements of Kingswear on the opposite shore, the roofs and towers stretch up above the houses, demanding recognition.

The Royal Naval College looks over the town of Dartmouth

The Britannia Naval College is, of course, a naval establishment, and therefore only rarely open to civilians but, in 1971, I had the opportunity of spending several weeks within its walls and got a privileged insight on the workings of our premier naval academy.

At the time, I was working as a producer for the regional ITV company, Westward, and went to the college to film a documentary that would show what goes into the making of a British naval officer. As it was to be shown during the year in which Prince Charles was about to become a student there, it offered the added bonus of also getting a brief glimpse of the training that would help that young man prepare for his role as king!

Over a period of eight months, we filmed the naval officer cadets at work and play: on manoeuvres over Dartmoor, putting classroom theory into practical experience on the bridge of their own seagoing training ship, enjoying the lavish hospitality of the Mess on Ladies' Night, and suffering the raw edge of a warrant officer's voice on the parade ground. Towards the end of our filming, I came to the conclusion that like most of our service academies, Dartmouth is one of the last

During the summer, Dartmouth is immensely popular and the ancient Butterwalk is always bulging with streams of visitors; Dartmouth Castle stands sentinel over the entrance of the River Dart

bastions of gracious living, a place where young men of the twentieth century can enjoy the trappings of a privileged lifestyle, from one hundred years ago, in which butlers and waiters are commonplace, while good manners and a respect for authority are a way of life.

At the end of the summer term, the College prepared for its Passing-Out Parade when the newly-commissioned officers were formally accepted into the ranks of serving men and able to take up their first official postings. Lord Louis Mountbatten had been invited to take the salute, and I had four film crews to capture the highlights of the day as the finale to the film. Three crews were 'on the ground' around the parade square, and one, a lone cameraman, sat in the crow's nest above the College clock tower, from where he had a superb

bird's-eye view of the day's proceedings. If Lord Louis was aware of the cameras as he walked up and down the lines of blue uniforms, making his inspection, or standing on the official dais while the officers, cadets, and Royal Marine Band marched past in salute, he never once showed it. But halfway through the afternoon, I got a message from one of his aides. 'Lord Louis says make sure that man doesn't fall out of the clock tower – it would make a terrible mess of the ceremony.'

A few years later I was back in Dartmouth with

From the quayside at Dartmouth, you look across the river to Kingswear ; the Kingswear ferry leaves the marina behind and plies steadily backwards and forwards carrying local people and visitors all the year round

another film crew, only this time it was the BBC, and I was only there as an observer – it was Chris, my husband, who was doing the work. At the time, the Beeb were filming sequences for that marvellous series *The Onedin Line*, and although the story was set in nineteenth-century Liverpool, the old wharves and warehouses of Dartmouth were so little changed from that period, when the town itself was a major seafaring port, that it made a perfect film set. A girlfriend of mine had been asked to find two dozen or so local men who would be prepared to act as 'extras' for a scene in which a group of young men were set upon by a pressgang. Chris and a few of his friends thought it would be good for a laugh, so volunteered their services.

He was asked not to shave for two days, and when he arrived on the set at 7.30 a.m. he was dressed in ragged breeches, a dirty shapeless calico shirt, and battered tricorn hat. He was one of the pressgang, and when the make-up artist had finished with him, adding even more shadow to his natural stubble, he looked a right villain. He and the rest of the 'gang' were rehearsed over and over again for their bit of action. They had to chase a hapless young recruit along the quayside, down a flight of steps to a small landing stage, and then stand over him, threatening and menacing, brandishing long vicious-looking staffs.

Eventually the scene was filmed, the extras paid off and told the date of transmission for 'their' episode, and we waited each Sunday night throughout that winter for the relevant story to be screened.

At last, there they were, chasing across the quay, and then Christopher's starring moment – a big close-up as he advanced down the steps. He was terrific! But I have to admit that we were probably the only two people who appreciated the scene. Not only was it all over in an eye-blink, but the make-up girls had done such a good job on him that not one of our friends who were watching that week recognised him!

Dartmouth is a yachtsman's haven, and there is a persistent clanking of the yachts' rigging near the river

Like most of Devon's rivers, the Dart has many moods and many characters. It springs to life among the windswept granite tors of Dartmoor, as two tributaries – the East and West Dart – which twist and turn in a frenzy of clear, bubbling water over moorland boulders and gravel, to join forces at the appropriately named Dartmeet.

From there, it meanders at a leisurely pace through the quiet meadows of ancient Buckfast Abbey, skirting the borders of Dartington Hall, ripples under the trees at Stoke Gabriel, and finally joins forces with the sea at Dartmouth.

It's amazing the number of places you can discover when you're engaged to someone who plays rugby. The village of Stoke Gabriel, on the banks of the River Dart, is a perfect example. For years, the V and A pub at Stoke Gabriel (the Victoria and Albert) was a regular haunt of all the rugby players in the area, and Christopher – now my husband – was no exception. But after two seasons of seeing only the car park and bar of the local pub, we decided that Stoke Gabriel must have something more to offer – so we dropped in one lunchtime, and were delighted by what we found.

It is a place where cottages rub shoulders with each other in the companionship of country life, and all roads lead to the river. If you enjoy the peace and quiet of country churchyards, you'll find the one at Stoke Gabriel especially attractive, and it offers by far the best view of the river, which at this point along its course is calm and tree-lined, and a haven for herons.

What a contrast just two miles up-river at Totnes, where the river is deep enough to house a commercial dock and has a small boat building industry. This old town is one of the British Council of Archaeology's top forty 'gem' towns. It is always full of the bustle and colour of a busy market place and, in the 15th and 16th centuries, it was second in the county only to Exeter in trading importance. Then, the port and a thriving cloth industry were the money-earners; today, its industries include dairy products and sweet-making.

Brixham and Berry Head

At the turn of the century when the Brixham fishing fleet moored within the safety of the tiny protected harbour, there were so many chunky little boats, topped with graceful masts and a maze of rigging, that you could barely see the colour of the water. The harbour remains one of the safest, and prettiest, in Devon. There is still a successful fishing industry in Brixham, and the fish market is fun to visit.

Brixham is full of history : in 1688, William of Orange first set foot on English soil here and there is a statue to commemorate his arrival. There is a replica of the Mayflower, *the tiny vessel that carried the Pilgrim Fathers across the Atlantic to America, which lies at rest in the harbour.*

When Chris and I were engaged, he lived on the outskirts of Brixham, not far from the cliffs of Berry Head. The great spur of rock juts out into the channel with the sweep of Torbay behind. It was our favourite place for a Sunday afternoon walk with his family's old Red Setter. Whatever the season, there's always a strong breeze on the Head, tugging at your hair and making your cheeks tingle and glow with its freshness. The old dog would busy himself chasing elusive rabbits through the brambly undergrowth, leaving the restless sea and the big empty sky to us, and the wheeling seagulls.

The Cathedral City of Exeter

Exeter Cathedral is such a tantalising building. It stands square and bold on the skyline when you enter the city from Dartmoor, and if you pause long enough on the brow of Haldon Hill on the A38, the cathedral towers are unmistakable in the centre of a sprawl of tower blocks, gas holders and sloping suburban roofs. It looks so accessible – but the closer you get, the more elusive it becomes, almost hiding its ornate gothic lines behind the twentieth-century shopping centre. But just slip through one of the narrow passages leading into Cathedral Close – and there it sits in splendid isolation – surrounded by green lawns, cobbled streets and Tudor houses. Nearby, one of the early bishops, Richard Hooker, keeps his silent vigil over the whole scene.

An afternoon's steady walk around Exeter can take you on a journey back through history to the time of the Romans – if, that is, you can manage to ignore the modern motor car!

The Regency elegance of Southernhay is just a few steps away from the exquisite mediaeval and Tudor houses and courtyards of Cathedral Square. At the Maritime Museum, you can cross the River Exe for 1 penny on a hand-drawn ferry and enjoy boats – ancient and modern – from all over the world.

The tall, narrow arch at the top of Castle Street leads into the courtyard of the Old Castle and an attractive archway of wrought-iron crosses one of the lanes leading to Cathedral Close.

The houses that cling to the steep sides of Stepcote Hill have hardly changed at all since Drake, Hawkins and Frobisher were regular visitors to the city.

Sidmouth

Sidmouth hardly looks like a source of great inspiration for a young journalist with its elegant Regency homes, and sedate, pretty seafront. But I know I learnt more about how to earn my living as a writer after one afternoon in that town than I'd learnt previously in six years as a reporter and broadcaster. My teacher was the writer R. F. Delderfield – the author of many immensely popular books, including A Horseman Riding By *which was recently serialised on television.*

Ron lived in an attractive thatched house on the cliffs overlooking the town. From the french windows in his circular study – the Gazebo – at the end of the house, we could look out over the sea. We talked for more than two hours, though the interview was to run for barely 15 minutes. I lapped up every word, and treasured his advice, and still hope that one day I may do it justice.

Cotehele House

Everyone of us, no doubt, has a selection of memories that are special to Christmas, whether it's decorating the tree, wrapping up the presents and watching the joy on children's faces when they're opened on Christmas morning, or just the pleasure of sharing seasonal good-will with loved ones. My own memories include curling up beside a huge log fire while a blizzard raged outside, skiing the best and longest run of my life down the side of the Italian Alps, and spending half an hour watching Cavaliers and Roundheads perform the ritual of battle drill in the teeth of a howling gale and pouring rain.

That last, somewhat bizarre Christmas memory occurred in the grounds of Cotehele house on the Sunday before Christmas Day in 1979. Cotehele is, for my money, the loveliest manor house in Cornwall. It rests comfortably in the crook of an arm of land that leans out into the River Tamar. In 1353, when Hilaria de Cotehele married William Edgcumbe, the whole house was part of her dowry. Several generations of Edgcumbes lived there until the fifteenth century when they moved into the 'modern' Tudor home overlooking Plymouth Sound, Mount Edgcumbe House. So Cotehele survived any extensive modernisation and is now safely in the hands of the National Trust.

It's not a large or magnificently grand house. It's a comfortable family home, a place where you expect to hear children playing in the woods or tumbling across the lawns, with parents indulgently looking down from the mullioned windows or watching from the gravel path. It's a gem of a house, blessed with timeless grace and elegance.

Whenever Chris and I are visited by friends or relatives who've never been to our corner of the South West, Cotehele is high on the list of 'places you *must* see before you go' and I've never passed up an opportunity to use the house and gardens as a location for films. It's been a stage for spring fashions, a living set for a gardening programme, and the backdrop for the dramatisation of a poem.

When the National Trust took over in 1947, they renovated some of the buildings, including the pretty

Cotehele, for me the loveliest manor house in Cornwall

circular dove cote, and the great barn which now houses one of the Trust's gift shops, and a first-class restaurant where, in the weeks before Christmas, they serve traditional festive meals. It's a marvellous way to enjoy a huge family pre-Christmas lunch – all that lovely food, and no washing up, plus the bonus of being able to walk off the effects of eating too much with an after-lunch stroll through the woods and along the river to Cotehele Quay.

There were eighteen of us for lunch that Sunday and although it was raining pretty heavily when we arrived,

we couldn't believe that it would go on pouring all through the afternoon – but it did. When we emerged after mountainous helpings of wonderful plum pudding and Cornish clotted cream, it was, as we say, 'chucking it down'.

So – no walk through the woods. Instead, we made a dash through the puddles on the cobbled courtyard for a glimpse of the Great Hall. Throughout the year, the walls are hung with armour and ancient weapons giving an accurate, but rather bleak picture of baronial living. But at Christmas time, the hall is warmed by the glow of an enormous open log fire and transformed with garlands of foliage and flowers that are slung from the roof, or draped over the candle chandeliers and the breastplates.

While we were all admiring the effect of the garlands and enjoying the heat of the fire, the great oak door swung open and there, in cloak and topboots, stood a Cavalier. In that vaulted room, surrounded by the trappings of the sixteenth and seventeenth centuries, he looked perfectly at home and, for a second, it was as if we, in our twentieth-century clothes, were the time travellers who'd blundered into *his* world – not the other way around.

This was not one of the famous Cotehele ghosts, however. He was, he explained, one of a group of young people who were members of the Sealed Knot, the band

The Great Hall with walls hung with armour ; Cotehele Quay, and the attractive circular dovecote

and the measured, practised tones of the Captain of the Guard. The fact that Cotehele probably never experienced a battle between the men of King and Parliament didn't seem to matter.

The nearest they seem to have come to a skirmish was in the reign of Richard III almost two hundred years before the Civil War. The master of Cotehele at that time, Richard Edgcumbe, swore allegiance to Henry Tudor, and not King Richard III, so the King's men were sent to capture Edgcumbe and bring him to trial. But he escaped by running through the woods towards the river, and taking refuge in a large tree that overhung the river. He weighted his hat with a stone, threw it into the water, and then watched his would-be captors ride away – assuming that Edgcumbe had fallen into the water and drowned. Instead, he fled to Britanny, and returned in 1485 to fight with the Tudor army at Bosworth. When Henry Tudor became Henry VII, Richard was rewarded with a knighthood, and later built a small chapel at Cotehele, on the spot where he'd been so nearly captured.

During the Civil War, the Edgcumbes again stayed loyal to the Crown, but it was the main family property, Mount Edgcumbe House, across the water from parliamentarian Plymouth, which suffered attack and siege, leaving Cotehele largely untouched. Nevertheless, our mock army persevered with their Cromwellian drill until their top boots were sodden, their woollen cloaks weighed heavy with water, and the rain fell in steady drips from the rims of their fine plumed hats onto their noses. Even the Royalist standard was too thoroughly soaked to flutter.

It was a brave display, much appreciated by all of us who stood relatively warm and dry under cover. But it occurred to me, as they trooped off, a wet and sorry band of foot soldiers, that, location apart, we'd probably just seen a more accurate demonstration of what it was really like to be a soldier for Parliament or King in that sorry war, than any of the intricately staged noisy battles performed with such relish in the summertime on the playing fields of England.

of enthusiasts who re-enact battles from the Civil War with amazing accuracy – and ferocity. They had planned to entertain the lunchtime revellers with a mock battle between Roundheads and Cavaliers on the lawns outside the house. But because of the atrocious weather, the battle was off. Instead, they offered to perform part of their musket drill in the cobbled yard.

So we left the comfort of the fire, and stood instead under the arch of the Gatehouse that leads to the main house. Out in the rain, the young men and women were draped in the colourful, cumbersome garb of the opposing armies, their leather jackets and helmets, the plumed hats and murderous pikestaffs all looking remarkably genuine. They drilled to the beat of a drum

Daphne du Maurier Country

It was while I was reading Frenchman's Creek *that I got my first 'glimpse' of the Helford River. It came not from standing on the water's edge, but through the wonderfully descriptive words of Daphne du Maurier. I could see beyond the mere words on the page and look into the quiet bay where the Frenchman hid his ship, and beyond to the sea where he dodged the British fleet and customs' men.*

Sometimes the picture you paint for yourself is so vivid that the real thing leaves you disappointed. But not the Helford. I slipped into the calm lapping water in a small motor boat that chugged out from Porth Navas to the oyster beds of the Helford. The river is like an ancient weathered tree, with its main trunk branching off to left and right into quiet, mysterious stretches of calm, flat water. The trees dip and curve from steep banks, trailing their leaves in the water, giving the river a soft, almost rounded shore line.

The oyster boat nudged its way into the deepest, widest part of the river where tall, willowy poles marked the beds. The oyster shells were dredged off the bottom and tipped into the boat, green with weed, gnarled by crustaceans, and smelling deliciously of the sea.

Later I drove around the estuary to Gweek and then to Mawgan, where at low tide the river shrinks to reveal the rich, food-filled mud of the estuary where the birds flock and feed. I especially love to watch the curlews and sandpipers at low tide. There's no rush and tumble with the Helford; it's a quiet river, lined with secret places. A river that's at peace with itself – and all who love it.

The Lizard Peninsula

The Lizard is the most southerly point of Great Britain. The road to Lizard Point runs straight and true across Goonhilly Downs, where the great dishes of the Earth Tracking station look like Salvador Dali sculptures on the flat, almost featureless, landscape. In contrast, the whole coastline is a honey-pot of delightful villages like Coverack and Porthallow, Cadgwith and Porth Mellin and Lizard itself. On a clear morning you can always smell the sea long before you see it, and hear it crashing tirelessly against the rocks. And when you finally look down from Lizard Point onto the rocks and white foam, it's not difficult to understand why the lifeboat slipway is such a common sight around the coastline.

If it hadn't been for Marconi, I don't suppose I would ever have discovered Porth Mellin. The great man sent the first radio message to America from the tiny hamlet of Poldhu, and I'd been dispatched to film a report on an anniversary of that historic occasion. Standing on the headland near the old radio station, and looking out across Mount's Bay, it was easy to see why Marconi chose this remote Cornish clifftop for his pioneering venture. As you look out across the waves, past the arm of Land's End, you can well believe that the sea stands empty all the way to the Americas. From my position on the cliffs, I could also make out the dozens of tiny coves and settlements nearby, and it was Porth Mellin that finally lured me down from my eyrie. It is a working village where the nets are hung out to dry on the quay side, and the lobster and crab pots are baited and stacked, ready to be dropped on the fishing grounds in the bay and there's nothing so good as real Cornish crab and lobster.

St Michael's Mount

When a 61,000-ton Liberian-registered tanker hit the Seven Stones Reef off Land's End on the morning of Saturday 18 March 1967, ripping a hole in her side, her cargo of crude oil began seeping oh so slowly into the sea. Within hours, it was spreading its evil stain across the waves and by mid-afternoon, it was clear that a full-scale disaster was about to hit the Cornish coastline. One hundred and twenty thousand tons of oil spewed out unchecked, hour after hour. In the days that followed, hundreds of thousands of seabirds perished, and as the tanker left her black, foul signature on the cliffs and beaches of Cornwall, her name was printed indelibly on the minds of all West Countrymen – *Torrey Canyon*.

Within hours, emergency services were preparing to spray the sea with chemicals to break up the slick, rescue as many seabirds as possible, and protect harbours and beaches with floating booms while the media mustered their reporters and cameramen to cover the biggest story in the region for years. At eight o'clock

The fairy-tale castle of St Michael's Mount against a dawn sky ; early riders take advantage of an empty beach

on Saturday evening, I had a telephone call from the BBC news editor telling me to be on Penzance Quay at 8.30 the next morning, to compile a report for that evening's news bulletin.

As I drove over the Tamar Bridge in the half-light of dawn, I switched on the BBC' six o'clock radio news for the latest report on the oil slick which was threatening to come ashore along the Penzance Peninsula and was already over eighteen miles long and two miles wide. The report spoke of a flotilla of small boats, backed up by an army of council workmen, all attacking the advancing, ever-growing blanket of oil. But the report in no way prepared me for the sight that greeted me as I drove along the A.30, over the rise out of the village of Crowlas and got my first glimpse of Mount's Bay.

I'd always thought of this as one of the prettiest sights in the county, with the coastline curving away to the left, the roofs of Penzance and Newlyn grey and slightly out of focus against the far hillside and, sitting in the centre of the bay, as perfect as a tea-time blancmange, the fairy-tale castle of St Michael's Mount.

When sea and sky are split by the image of an island, I find the view it presents is always at least interesting, at best spectacular. So it is with Mount's Bay. When the sky is streaked crimson and gold with the embers of a dying sunset, or blackened with the clouds of an Atlantic storm, or even when it's just a flat featureless grey, barely streaked with the silver of dawn, St Michael's Mount stands strongly in the foreground with the towers and balustrades of the castle a sharp and constant silhouette against the changing backdrop.

The causeway leading to the Mount, and the imposing castle with its tower and balustrades

On that Sunday morning, the Mount looked just as pretty as ever, but its setting was tarnished. The whole bay was streaked with the glossy, iridescent strips of *Torrey Canyon* oil which flattened the waves as though trying to smother the life out of the sea. Even the sky was subdued and yellow in sympathy. One small fishing boat bobbed steadily in the middle of the mire, spraying chemicals onto the surface. It struck me that it was probably like trying to clean out a cesspit with an eye dropper – but at least the clean up was underway.

I spent the whole of that day talking to officials and experts about the danger to Cornish beaches, the threat to the holiday industry, the various chemicals and methods available to attack the oil on the surface, and the vital question of how to stop the flow of oil at source. There had never been an accident quite like this before, and everyone concerned was breaking new ground.

By lunchtime, it was clear that apart from the damage the oil would do to the landscape and commercial interest in the county, the threat to seabirds was appalling. The divers, like razorbills, and guillemots, were at greatest risk. As they plunged under the surface, their bodies were coated with oil. Those that didn't drown and suffocate would try to preen the sticky mess out of their feathers, only to die horribly as the oil burnt their intestines.

I walked along Marazion beach with cameraman Jon Wooldrige and watched as RSPCA officials and volunteers tried manfully to rescue birds as they were washed ashore. A few guillemots looked ill and confused in a large cardboard box, while others lay in pathetic black heaps, hardly recognisable as birds, all along the shoreline. We saw a guillemot struggling in the oily surf. It went under twice and was scooped up by a rescuer's net. The body convulsed, one wing jerked aimlessly, and it was dead in seconds. For weeks, that scene was repeated around the coastline as thousands of birds perished.

I felt sick, and helpless, and angry. And I wasn't alone. We took a small boat out across the oily waters to the Mount. The spring bulbs were about to burst, and

the early primulas splashed the hillside with colour but I'm afraid they were given scant attention. Inside the castle, Lord and Lady St Levan looked out on the scene around them with sad, disbelieving eyes. They had watched the first fingers of pollution creep over the horizon into Mount's Bay, then gradually spread its hand until what seemed like a solid blanket advanced on the Mount, surrounded them, and then passed on towards the shore. The cliffs were already littered with dead and dying birds, and Lady St Levan was particularly anxious for a family of gulls that had nested year after year on the same ledge outside the dining-room window. As we looked out on that depressing scene, I'm sure that we all thought that within days the entire coastline would be plastered in black, sticky oil, and that parts of Cornwall would never be quite the same again.

As I've said, nothing like that had happened before, and no one was sure what the long-term effects of a major spillage of oil would be.

Well, all that was over fifteen years ago. Last spring, I stood on the battlements of the castle looking out over the same scene, with the sun sparkling on the water, the cliffs washed clean by the waves, and the name *Torrey Canyon* nothing more than a bad memory.

I'd gone back to the Mount in the spring to make a programme about the island community for the BBC 2 series, *In the Country*. This time, I arrived not by boat, but horse – a 'white charger' on loan from a local stable

The Mount is completely isolated from the mainland at high tide ; then is the time to relax on Marazion beach

to simulate the arrival of Sir Trevillion, one of King Arthur's knights, and of early pilgrims who'd been crossing the sands from Marazion beach at low tide since before the Middle Ages, to pay homage at a site where St Michael appeared in a vision to local fishermen.

In springtime, the Mount is a delight. Although it stands battered on all sides by sea and winds, the climate is, for the most part, surprisingly stable and mild. Amongst the trees on the steep narrow paths up to the castle, the spring flowers hug the rock face in clumps of blue and yellow, scarlet and white, shielded from the wind by evergreens and shrubs. Even on the seaward side of the island, where the Mount stands full face to the wind, the head gardener was able to show me a cliff-side garden where shrubs and herbaceous borders bloomed and thrived, all cleverly protected by walls and stout hedges from the burning, drying salt winds.

There are numerous small island communities around our coast and I've always found that people who live on them are a breed apart. They have a strong sense of independence, and community, plus a genuine pride in 'their' land which they demonstrate by extending a warmth and friendliness towards those who visit their home. John Matthews, the senior guide on St Michael's

Mount, embodies all those qualities. He has the weathered face, the strong capable hands and unruffled calm of a man who has lived off the sea all his life, and he's genuinely proud of the unique, almost magical Mount he calls home.

When I arrived on a Friday evening in late April, the stark, clean rays of the sun had lit the castle and harbour to look like a Hollywood film set, and we were all confident of glorious weather for the next two days' shooting. Overnight, the wind came up and, by morning, we were working in the teeth of a force nine gale. One of our heavy electronic cameras was blown over by the strength of the gusts, the floor manager Cliff, was knocked off his feet, and John and I had to struggle with our heads down into an invisible force field to walk from the gun batteries to the main castle entrance on the west side of the Mount.

And then it rained. Not just the gentle rain of spring, which we could have lived with, but a sheet of water that advanced across the bay and deposited its burden in a torrential downpour. We consoled ourselves with the knowledge that although we were wind-battered and numb with cold, the rest of the West Country was being snowed on. So we dodged the wind, dashed in and out between showers, and finished recording on time, and as far as we were concerned, we had a smashing pro-gramme and the visit had been a great success.

But the islanders were genuinely upset. Lord St Levan and his gentle wife kept reassuring us that 'it isn't always like this – honestly', and as far as John Matthews was concerned, the weather had demon-strated appalling bad manners to their guests.

By the time we left, we'd all been touched by the magic of the place in spite of the weather, and as I got into the small boat to motor back to the mainland, John gave me a neat package. At home, I opened it and found a tiny porcelain vase in the shape of a boot, with a transfer of spring flowers and the legend 'St Michael's Mount' across the top. It sits on my dressing-table at home in Devon, and every spring I make sure it's filled with muscari and primula – just to make it feel at home.

Mousehole

When it comes to Art, I'm afraid I'm what the experts regard as the archetypal Philistine, in that I don't know much about it, but I know what I like.

And what I *don't* like are surrealist blobs and *avant garde* abstracts. So when I went to the village of Mousehole in Cornwall to meet artist Jack Pender, I don't know who was more apprehensive – him or me.

Jack paints boats. Not the sort that you would recognise immediately as the small clinker-built fishing vessels, at rest in the mud of the tiny harbour at Mousehole. His 'boats' were coloured bananas, skewered with cocktail sticks, suspended against a block of pure colour. Not my cup of tea at all, but amongst people who know about these things, they're regarded as vibrant, excitingly original and highly collectable.

Jack was to be the subject of one of my *Rippon Report* programmes for BBC Plymouth. We sat and talked in the window seat of his diminutive fisherman's cottage, looking out over the harbour towards the arms of the breakwater, which feature in many of his paintings. In one, he shows them simply as two oblongs of black against a white background. I could understand the symbolism, but preferred what I actually saw with my simple, non-artistic eye, in the same way that I preferred the painting of the harbour, done by Jack's grandfather on a piece of lovingly-framed cardboard which hung above the fireplace. It was overflowing with square whitewashed houses, and small boats that jostled and bobbed for room in the harbour and had all the simplistic charm of a Grandma Moses picture.

After two days together, Jack and I agreed to differ. I'm afraid I didn't become one of his converts – at least, not where painting was concerned, but the experience wasn't entirely wasted. For what I did begin to appreciate was the strength and spirit of comradeship that makes a small, independent community like Mousehole so strong and resilient. Jack is a true Mousehole man, with salt in his veins, and eyes that look ever seaward. His father and

grandfather and the Penders before them, were all fishermen. And although Jack hasn't followed them into the boats and onto the sea to make his living, his work is dominated by them.

At lunchtime, the men of Mousehole gathered in the bar of the Ship Inn to sink pints and swop yarns, their faces permanently tanned, and split with the grins and laughter-lines of contented men.

The collecting box on the bar and the photographs on the walls bore witness to the strong links between the men, the sea and the lifeboat service. I was introduced around the room amid the usual public bar din of back slapping and leg pulling. There was a discernible note of pride in the look and the voice of the man next to me when he nudged me in the ribs and pointed across the room to say, "'E's in the lifeboat, so's 'e, and so's 'e' – the last indication being to the man behind the bar – landlord Charlie Greenhaugh. It was noisy in the pub,

The picturesque village and harbour of Mousehole ; the Ship Inn where pints are sunk and yarns are swapped

but it was the noise of comradeship. These men had scrapped with each other in the school playground, married each other's sisters and cousins, cast their nets within hailing distance of their neighbour's on the fishing grounds, and would see out eternity with their gravestones rubbing shoulders in the church yard. Mine was a brief familiarity in their midst – but a happy one.

It's impossible to drive your car through every street in the village. The irregular shapes of the houses and yards fit into each other like a complicated jig-saw, and the roads that separate them were made wide enough for people, not wheels, so it's only by walking that you can

The harbour is peaceful and the far side of Mount's Bay is just visible in the soft light of dawn

enjoy the charm of the higgledy-piggledy streets, and discover the 'sights' of the place. Like Dolly Pentreath's cottage, the home of the woman said to be the last person in Cornwall to speak the true Cornish language. She died in 1777, and although there are still people who learn and speak the old tongue, they do so as an academic exercise, rather than a way of life.

Walk just a few yards up the hill from Dolly Pentreath's, and you'll find all that remains of Keigwin Manor, the only building to survive when the village was burned and sacked by the Spanish fleet in 1595. It was a reprisal. A hit-and-run mugging for the part the village had played in defeating the Spanish Armada

The charm of the higgledy-piggledy streets, and the houses which fit into each other like a complicated jigsaw ; the harbour at rest, waiting for a new day.

seven years earlier. Then, a local man Thomas Fleming had sailed to Plymouth in his boat, the *Golden Hind*, to warn Drake that the Spanish Fleet had been sighted off the Scillies. When the Spanish returned to take their revenge, Thomas Fleming's grandfather, Jenkin Keigwin, stayed to defend his home and died in the process, sword in hand. The sword is now in the museum at Penzance, and the house stands as a reminder of the only occasion when the invading

Spanish Army actually landed on British soil.

I know all this because Jack's mother, Nettie Pender, has written a history of the village. She was seventy when she sat down to record her 'recollections' and wrote with a painstaking eye for detail, and genuine love of her home.

It became something of a standing joke between Jack and myself that on one of my return visits to his studio, I would take my husband Chris, who, like me, is a 'lover of fine art'! And it so happened that we were both in Cornwall at the end of December in 1981, and drove to the village to make the promised 'social call'. It was Wednesday 30 December. The harbour was decked out with Christmas decorations, the streets were lit with raw winter sunshine, but the houses wore widows' weeds.

On 19 December, the Penlee lifeboat, the *Solomon Browne*, had sunk with all hands when going to the aid of the freighter, *Union Star*. On the day we drove into Mousehole, unknown to us, they were preparing to bury one of her crew – the landlord Charlie Greenhaugh. Jack had been made an executor of the disaster fund, and had been called away to a meeting. Chris and I knew we couldn't stay. Although we were greeted with cheery 'hellos' as we walked along the quay, we both felt like intruders, and didn't want to be thought of like the ghouls, who turn up at the scene of an accident, to stand and stare.

Our admiration for the courage and dedication of those men and their community is enormous – but that wasn't the time to express it. So we turned the car back along the coastal road to Newlyn, promising to return later in the summer, to enjoy Jack's 'banana' boats and the special atmosphere of that resilient, independent community.

Minack Theatre

Although Cornwall is famous as a holiday resort and its more popular beaches are crowded in the summer, there are still glorious stretches of sand that always manage to feel deserted. The beach at Porthcurno on the Land's End Peninsula is a good example. The long sweep of golden sand is backed and protected by a wall of cliffs that make a perfect sun trap.

Perched high above on the cliff edge, looking out across the ever-changing sea, is the magical bowl of the Minack Theatre. This fairy-tale theatre was hewn out of the rocks in 1932 by the redoubtable Miss Dorothy Cade, aided by her gardener and just a handful of helpers. The theatre, built at the bottom of Miss Cade's clifftop garden, was originally a small affair – somewhere to stage a village production of A Midsummer Night's Dream. Now, its appearance could rival that of any Grecian amphitheatre, and the productions range from Shakespeare to musicals, comedy to ballet.

There's only one possible drawback – the English weather, and more than once I've suffered a soaking from an unwelcome summer shower in the middle of a performance. But, on a warm still summer's night, you can look beyond the action on the stage to the sea, the cliffs and the setting sun, listen to Prospero call up the tempest and watch the sky respond with its own spectacular pattern of clouds and lightning – believe me, there's not a theatre in the West End to rival it.

Land's End

Whoever coined the old weather lore rhyme, 'Red sky at night, sailor's delight' must, at some time in his life, have stood on the very tip of England, at Land's End, looking out across the sea towards the Longships lighthouse: the original lighthouse was built in 1795 but the present building dates from 1883. It stands about a mile offshore and the Wolf Lighthouse, built in 1869, is eight miles away.

In the summer and early autumn, the sky plays unbelievable tricks with the light and cloud patterns, turning the western skies into a riot of streaked gold and orange, purple and red. The patterns on the sand at Sennen Beach, about a mile away, would do credit to Dali or Picasso when the sunset floods the whole bay with a phenomenal spectrum of light.

A Cliff-edge Mine

It was a gem of a day. One of those occasions between Christmas and New Year when the weather forgets that it's supposed to be damp and wintery, and teases with the promise of an early spring. Chris and I were enjoying the freedom of a few days' winter holiday, and we'd gone to the far west corner of the Cornish peninsula to West Penwith, to revisit some of our favourite haunts. The car radio was giving a traffic warning of severe weather in parts of Devon and Cornwall. But, as we looked up to a clear blue sky and felt the gentle warmth of the December sunshine, we decided they were obviously talking about another planet, and headed the car towards the village of St Just and the site of the ancient tin mines clinging to the cliffs at Botallack.

I'd come here first on a November evening in 1965 as a newspaper reporter to write a feature on the Count House Folk Music Club. Although all mining had ceased in the area in the early 1900s, many of the buildings had survived, and a group of talented musicians and singers, including the melodious, capacious Brenda Wootten, had established a folk club in the Count House. It had rapidly become something of a mecca for folk fans at a time when that brand of music was all the rage.

It was dusk when I drove towards the village, guided in by the cluster of lights that sat, isolated, in the middle of a sea of night-blackened fields. Through the sudden brightness of the village and out onto a road that was little more than a track, I followed the club posters indicating the way. My headlights picked out piles of rock and ruined buildings and eventually the Count House itself, a long, single-storey building that had been the main office for the mine. Music and light spilled out into the darkness through tall narrow windows and the ever-open barn door.

Inside, the whitewashed walls were hung with ubiquitous fishing nets, and every inch of space was crammed with the foot-tapping, sing-along faithful. Lusty voices were raised in unison to old favourites like 'Haul 'Em Away' and 'Johnny, I Hardly Knew Ye', and

hushed in deference while Brenda sang the haunting 'Lamorna'. The whole evening was captured on tape, and later released as an L.P. So while my own offering in print in the following Sunday's newspaper probably ended up lighting fires or wrapping fish and chips, the music from that night is still very much alive.

But it wasn't the music that subsequently brought me back to this corner of Cornwall again and again. It was the mystery of standing outside the Count House that evening, in the pitch black of night, and just being able to make out the weird shapes of arches and chimney stacks, of ruined engine houses and abandoned spoil tips, and hear the crash and swoosh of the sea somewhere below me. It was like being in a darkened room with unfamiliar noises and objects, and I wanted to

St Just village, which once housed a community of families who drew a bare living wage from the tin mines of Botallack, is now a place in which to feel at home

switch on a light and get my bearings. So it was curiosity that took me back on a second visit in daylight, just two years later, and a sense of wonder and the visual enjoyment of what I found that has drawn me there ever since.

St Just is not a pretty village. Its diminutive square houses were built of natural stone on simple practical lines to house a community of families who drew a bare living wage from the mines and had never experienced the niceties or comforts of wealth. But what it lacks in looks, it makes up for in character. It's a comfortable, cosy place without pretentions. A place to feel at home in, even if you're a stranger. The main square is presided over by a clock tower and leaves you spoilt for choice in the collection of pubs offering good beer and good food.

Faced with the unexpected bonus of springtime in December, Chris and I were loth to go inside any of them, but an early start, and a five-hour exposure to the crisp Cornish air, had left us ravenous. In a bar that was low-ceilinged and wood-warmed, we feasted on turkey pie and chips. As I was about to clear my plate, one of the locals appeared carrying a tea plate covered with a red paper serviette. 'A few home-made mince pies,' he said quietly. 'Just a small thank you from me to you for the pleasure you bring into my house with your programmes.'

The Count House, once the main office of the mine, now stands aloof from the rubble and ruins of the cliff edge

There are times when I am left speechless by the kindness of total strangers, and this was one of them. The pies were delicious, and the generosity of the thought made them even sweeter. When we rose to leave, our benefactor asked if we'd like to see inside a 'real old Cornish miner's cottage'. We were only too happy to accept, and were led out of the back door of the pub, past the empty beer crates in the yard, to the front door of his home which was one of the neat little houses that faced onto the square. Inside, it was tiny. Just six strides could take you from one side to the other of the single downstairs room. Our host explained that originally the downstairs had been divided into two rooms, and it was frankly impossible to visualise how any family could have lived in such cramped circumstances.

We left the house, warmed by the friendliness of our welcome, and the promise of a 'cup of tea any time you're passing', and drove out of the village, heading north towards the sea. There are no green hedges in this part of Cornwall. Irregular-shaped fields are marked and boundaried by low stone walls fashioned in the coarse granite boulders that lie just below the thin turf and defy the use of the plough. I can never understand how the walls stay up, for the boulders aren't stuck together with either soil or cement, just perched one on top of another – an example of willpower as much as the builder's skill. Anywhere else, this profusion of stone would be harsh and out of place, but here the soft green of pastureland stumbles headlong into piles of granite waste and outcrops of mine waste tips. There are so many rocks that, against this treeless landscape, the stone walls are nothing more than veins, standing proud on a smooth skin.

We drove past the last of the green fields, along the narrow lane and parked in front of a tangle of briar and bricks. The Count House, now an attractive gourmet restaurant, stands back slightly from the rest of the workings, isolated by a clean sweep of gravel drive, and standing almost aloof and neat in the rubble and ruins that cover the cliff top.

In the 1860s, this spot was crowded with engine-houses and tramlines, sheds and winding-gear as the Botallack Mine had been one of the most profitable in the area. And when the tin ran out and arsenic took its place, a whole new set of buildings sprang up, including the labyrinth of chambers through which the arsenic was purified. Eventually, even arsenic couldn't show a profit so the mine was closed, and Nature began to reclaim her own. What wasn't knocked down, fell down, to be smothered in a camouflage of brambles and ferns.

The contrast from Cornish fields to industrial wasteland is abrupt, and the effect untidy. But once you've passed beyond the barrier of brambles and piles of half-covered masonry, what lies on the other side takes your breath away. A curving wall of granite cliffs drops a hundred feet or more down into the sea where the waves worry and nag themselves into a permanent froth on the tideline. Across the face of the cliff, one thin streak of bare earth marks the course of a footpath which leads to the far tip of the headland, and the two derelict skeletal engine-houses sit stark and incongruous on the rocks, like a pair of giant Leggo bricks, just stuck there for fun.

This was the Crown's section of the famous Botallack Mine and in the 1880s Cornishmen regarded this site as one of the mining wonders of the world with engine-houses, winding-gear and machinery perched precariously on slim ledges across the cliff face. The higher of the two buildings housed the winding-gear for the great Diagonal shaft which sank thirteen hundred feet *below* sea level and had workings which extended nearly half a mile under the waves beyond the cliffs. They say that when the men were working in the dark underground chambers, they could hear the waves crashing above them, but such was the skill of the Cornish engineers that the mine tunnels and shafts stayed as dry – though some say even drier – as any inland.

To walk down the path as we did that December day towards the old houses, is to walk, like Alice, into a

Cornwall has many spectacular cliffs and Cape Cornwall strikingly stands above the restless waves

world that's a little out of step with the rest of time. The images are slightly blurred. A pile of stones, or the square overgrown outline of a foundation, are the only clues to suggest what had been there a century before and what the area looked like when it rang to the tune of King Tin.

Chris and I leapt across the rocks to stand inside the nearest building. The stonework is still immaculate, and the windows look out on a scene of sky, sea and cliffs that hasn't changed in a thousand years. On the far side of the bay, the waves were crashing onto the rocks which looked black and featureless against the white glare of the sky, but their outline was softened by a layer of fine mist that rolled and eddied just above the surface. At first, I thought it was the sea spray being thrown up by the force of the waves, then I realised it was coming, not off the sea but off the land itself. Old miners used to believe that they could trace a tin lode from the surface on warm days, because the metal in the ground held the heat and released a fine heat haze. So perhaps that's what I was seeing, for certainly the far lip of the bay boasts at least four stacks that mark the site of old mine workings and, as every Cornishman knows, there's still plenty of tin left in Cornwall. Or maybe it was just a trick of the light – who knows?

All I do know is that no one who comes to this place can fail to be impressed by the wide scope of the big empty sea, the spectacle of waves exploding in jets of white spume at the foot of the cliffs, and the audacity of Man for calling Nature's bluff and building where she would least expect him to.

On our walk back up the steep hill, we often paused to get our breath back, and to take in the view. I'd like to think that the miners did the same. After a day below ground, working in the airless black of a mine shaft, with only pinpoints of candle light to pierce the gloom, it must have been good to close your eyes to the ugliness of an industrial site, and drink in the clean salt air, and the beauty of those Cornish cliffs.

Over small fields and sturdy walls to Cape Cornwall

An Artist's Paradise

When my father bought our first family car, it changed our lives completely. It was as if I'd spent the first part of my life in a pigeon loft and had suddenly had the doors thrown open with the invitation to 'fly little bird, fly'. Pedal power had brought the beaches of south Devon within my range – but a car opened up the whole peninsula. During that first year, we made weekend trips to scores of places that had previously been just names on the map, which is how I got my first introduction to the town of St Ives.

On a Friday in August, our little black Morris scuttled into a town that was bathed in the clear golden light of the afternoon sun. We located Johnson's Caravan Park, which was to be our holiday home for the week, and anticipated seven days' relaxation with sun, sea and sand. The next morning, it poured with rain – and it went on raining for the rest of that week on a scale that ranged from just damp and miserable to thoroughly wet and nasty.

The cinema and twice-weekly beetle drive in the church hall were dry havens for bedraggled holiday-makers like us and we seemed to spend a great deal of time in the newsagents, buying papers, magazines and books of crossword puzzles; or wandering through the town, or across the wet sands clad in the 'grockle's' uniform of a five-bob plastic mac.

And I think that's why I came to like the town so much. We discovered cobbled lanes and back yards, fishermen's lofts and tiny shops that would have been unknown to us if we'd lazed away each day on one familiar patch of sunny beach. With so much to explore, there wasn't time to resent the rain.

One afternoon we stumbled across an artist at work in a converted sail loft. St Ives, of course, is famous for its colony of painters and sculptors but, until then, I'd never actually seen any of them at work. His canvasses were stacked haphazardly around the walls or hanging on joists, while he sat in the middle of this colourful, untidy jumble, working at an easel.

St Ives town and harbour – an artist's paradise

The harbour, and some typical lanes in St Ives

On his right, an upturned tea-chest was crammed with a collection of jam jars sprouting brushes, a tangle of twisted paint tubes oozing colour, and a pile of oil-stained rags. In a semi-circle around him, the floor was spattered with splashes of paint which formed a multi-coloured border between him and us. As we walked, cat-like, from canvas to canvas, not wanting to disturb him, he dabbed at a large seascape. My father was much taken with a view of the fishing boats in St Ives harbour. 'How much?' he asked. The figure quoted was more than he'd paid for our precious little car, so we left the loft discreetly, and bought postcards instead.

In subsequent years, we enjoyed many sun-scorched holidays in the town, but it became a place that I preferred to visit in the winter, when the streets were free of jostling holiday-makers and the sharp salt-tanged air rolled in with the Atlantic breakers to breathe life back into the community.

As a reporter, my work took me there on a number of occasions, especially in the late sixties when St Ives became a fashionable mecca for hippies. Many of the locals objected to their presence, and allowed their bitterness and resentment to spill out into public condemnation. But on a lighter note, I was sent by my editor to have flowers painted on me by one of the hippy artists. The girl drew brightly-coloured blooms and trailing leaves across my stomach and around my back – it was, I was told, the latest craze among the flower people to brighten up all those areas of bare flesh lying on the beach! I seem to remember that the paint brush

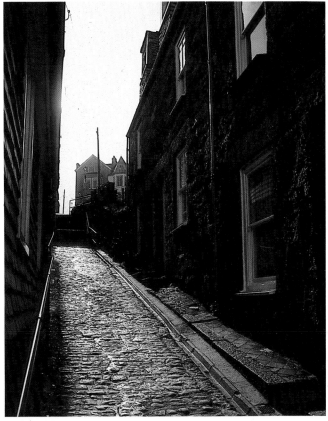

tickled almost unbearably, but it certainly made a colourful item for our nightly news magazine, and also moved one lady viewer to write a complaining letter to the BBC condemning me as a shameless hussy!

That interview was done at the height of the summer, and I doubt if the artist has ever been heard of since. In contrast, it was in the depths of winter, on a grey rain-washed day in January, that I met one of the world's great artists, the potter Bernard Leach. I'd been sent to interview him on his eightieth birthday in 1967. He was tall, I remember, in a suit that looked two sizes too large for him. Even the skin on his face was ill-fitting. It seemed to balance unsteadily on his brow and cheek bones, and was only pinned securely in place above his lips by the brittle grey of his moustache.

I must confess that previously I had never heard of Bernard Leach. At twenty-three, the esoteric world of pots had passed me by. But I'd done my research, and learnt of his work in Japan with that country's great artists, and of the skill and unique creativity he'd brought to his studio in St Ives. So I asked all the right questions and provided convenient platforms for him to extol and expand his theories on beauty and art. For twenty minutes, I looked into that wise old face and his gentle dark eyes. Eyes that held the wisdom of the east and a twinkle that suggested he knew he was talking to a Philistine! And he was right. For although I realised that I was obviously talking to a craftsman of some note, it was years before I fully appreciated just how great an artist he was, and although I may have been blasé at the time, I'm eternally grateful for the chance I had of meeting him – just once.

Redruth and Truro

On the long and often lonely drives from one end of the region to the other, there are landmarks that help to make the journey shorter – like the elegant spires of Truro Cathedral, the tallest of which rises 250 ft into the air. When they come into view, I know I'm only an hour and a half from home.

In truth, however, Truro is too nice a town to keep passing through without stopping and I often snatch a half-hour in the town to visit one of my favourite saddlery shops, or browse in the second-hand book shops and antique shops. In the 18th century, Truro became both a fashionable place for merchants to live and the centre of county society. As a result, it has some very elegant Georgian terraces and crescents that make Truro, for me, the most attractive town in Cornwall.

Built in the Early English style, visitors to the cathedral are often surprised to learn that it wasn't completed until 1910.

A few miles away, in Redruth, the Wesleyan Chapel holds special memories for me. I once compered a concert for the Four Lanes Male Voice Choir in that building. If you've never heard a Cornish *choir* – then you should. The sound is stupendous, and I can still feel my spine tingle, just at the thought of it.

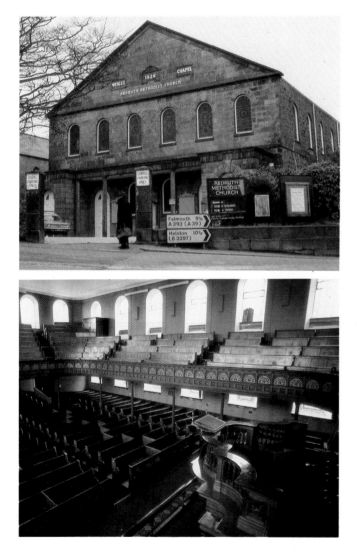

Cornwall's 'Royal' Show

When the magazine *Farmer's Weekly* named Cornwall's Royal Agricultural Show as Show of the Year in 1980, they were only confirming what people in the county had known for years.

For three days every June, the permanent site at Wadebridge offers the basic fare of most agricultural shows – an opportunity for farmer and stockman to show off their finest animals, a chance for the townie to mingle with the countryman and sample just a flavour of his way of life, and for those involved with trade in the county to fill their order books and boost business for the year ahead.

But there's an extra set of ingredients that has always made the 'Royal' rather special, and given it a very distinctive, unique and exciting atmosphere. For me, it comes from the great sense of community that exists in Cornwall. Before you arrive, you know you'll be meeting friends that you probably haven't seen since last year's show. They're a chauvinistic bunch, the Cornish – my friends there are always telling me I was 'born wrong side o' the Tamar' – and certainly the Royal provides them with an opportunity to put on an event that's seen as a showpiece for the very best that the county has to offer. A crucible for Cornish pride. Other show regulars would no doubt offer an entirely different formula but, whatever their reasons, they all add up to one thing, and that is that the Royal Agricultural is a show that's held in deep affection by the Cornish people – and maybe it's just that by itself that makes it so special.

During my early days in television, I had a regular date with the show on its opening day to provide a filmed package for the evening magazine programme. I suspect that one of the main reasons for sending me was because I lived in the country and it was therefore assumed that, unlike some of my colleagues, I knew the difference between a South Devon and a Charolais – but no matter, it meant I always got in free! Even when I no longer had to go there on duty, I needed very little persuasion to take a day off and go to the show for pleasure.

My first port of call is always the pig pens. 'Nasty smelly creatures – wouldn't go near them', is how many people react when I say that, but I genuinely like pigs, and think they are much-maligned creatures. They have a great sense of humour – at least, most of the ones I've met have – and seeing a hundred or more of them together sets me up for the day. I know many people visit the show ground and never go near the livestock judging rings but, for me, that's one of the main attractions.

I find it's incredibly soothing and relaxing just to lean on a fence and watch the white-coated handlers parade their stock around the bowler-hatted judges and stewards. The bull ring is especially soporific. No one in

At the 'Royal', the townie can mix with the countryman, and the farmer can show off his finest animals

the world can hurry several hundredweight of prize Hereford, so they make their way in regal stately procession around the arena, each beast stoically judging those who judge, and maintaining a majestic indifference to the critical eyes and occasional poke in the ribs. Why is it that when bulls walk, they always look as though their feet are killing them? To me, they look like women who are wearing shoes that are too tight with six-inch heels. They seem to teeter, painfully, on tip toe. But it says much for their character that they do so without ever losing their dignity.

Candy floss and curtains, silage and swimming pools, they're all part of the Royal, and no visit would be complete without at least an hour in the flower tent where the heady mixture of perfume and colour, and the artistry of growers and arrangers, always delights.

But as much as anything, it's the people who make the show, and the Royal really is thought of as a major social event in the county calendar.

An old friend of mine, who farms in Cornwall, has been a show 'regular' since he was a young lad, and he reckons that if he sat on the tailboard of his trailer behind the main ring for the three days of the show, he'd see the entire world and his wife go by. I must admit it does seem at times, when you stand in the middle of the main avenue and look out at a mass of heads and faces milling between the canvas stalls, that the whole county has turned out for the day, and on the one occasion that I led a young foal around the main ring in the Parade of Champions, I could hardly walk a dozen steps without recognising a friend or neighbour leaning on the rails – and nor could anyone else in the line-up.

Last year, I found myself in the main ring again. Not as an exhibitor, or even as a spectator, but as one of those people the competitors all love to hate – a judge.

I'd been asked to judge the regional finals of the Hermès Concours d'Elégance, a competition for horse-drawn carriages in which horse, carriage and rider must all be turned out to perfection. There were thirty-six entries in the class and, in each combination, the horses glowed from hours of grooming and attention, the carriages sparkled under coats of new paint and polish, while the drivers were living fashion plates with elegantly veiled and feathered hats, polished top boots, and very beautifully tailored clothes. I had to choose only six who would receive rosettes and one overall winner, although almost every entry was worthy of the title. Round and round they bowled, each one the epitome of elegance.

What a lonely, and agonising job it was being a judge,

knowing that whomever I chose at the end of the day, thirty-five people would be convinced that I was wrong. All I could do was to stick to the letter of the rules and choose the combination which achieved elegant perfection in *my* eyes. I called my winner into the centre of the arena – a magnificent blue carriage driven by a lady whose outfit matched the colour and period of the vehicle exactly and pulled by a horse who moved as though he knew he was a champion. The rest of the competitors looked disappointed, but the crowds applauded – and I thankfully walked out of the arena with the confidence of a judge who has just made a popular decision and knows she's not about to be lynched.

Some of the main attractions : a handsome pair show their paces, and hunt servants of the local beagle pack make their own unofficial judgement

Delabole

'Please, Mrs Brown, may I have a nature table in my bedroom?' The old lady regarded me solemnly over her folded arms and ample bosom. 'I could use the lid of the big box underneath the window,' I explained eagerly. I wanted a nature table so much.

She considered the idea a moment longer, and then agreed. 'All right, miss,' she said, 'but I keep the best blankets in that box, so you're not to have any water in your jam jars – I couldn't risk getting those things soaked.'

It occurred to me that without water none of the foxgloves and pennywort, the campions or slender seed-swollen grasses I'd already collected from the hedge-rows would last more than a day before dying. But after all, the lanes were full of replacements, so it was a small price to pay for the pleasure of having my own collection.

During the previous term at school, the nature table had been the centre of attention in our classroom, groaning under the weight of specimens, animal and vegetable, eagerly collected in matchboxes, nets and jam jars by my classmates.

'See if you can build up a nature table of your own during the summer holidays,' our teacher had suggested – and that's exactly what I was trying to do in Mrs Brown's miniature cottage in the north Cornish village of Delabole.

Doris Brown, and husband Henry, had been born, bred and married in that village where the yawning pit of the slate quarry was the focus of local employment, and pride, for it produced – and still does – some of the finest quality slate in the country. In fact, the whole village lived and died with slate. Their houses were faced with it, their graves marked by it, and in the small privy in the courtyard at the rear of the Browns' cottage you sat on it – as the seat was fashioned from a single grey slab of the smooth, fine-grained material.

The Browns had no children of their own so were among the first to offer homes to evacuee children from the bombed city of Plymouth. Which is how my Aunt Rose came to be packed off to Delabole in the spring of 1941. She became a surrogate daughter, returning after the war to spend summer holidays in the diminutive two-up two-down terraced cottage.

When I was four, I was allowed to accompany her for a few days as a 'treat', and for the next several years Delabole became a regular summer haunt, each stay for a few days, then weeks longer than the last.

Once inside that self-contained community, it was like being on an island. The rest of the world simply ceased to exist. The village children accepted me as an oddity. The 'townie' who dropped in for a few weeks every year. But I was invited to join their 'gang' and we'd skirmish through the tangle of weeds and scrub on the very lip of the great quarry – insulated by childish bravado and indifference to the dangers. We'd often act out the story of King Arthur and his Knights of the Round Table – for Arthur's legendary castle, Tintagel, was after all less than half a morning's walk away on a beautiful piece of Cornwall's coastline.

Delabole, one of the largest slate quarries in England

But it was the fields and lanes embracing the village that became my favourite haunt. They were full of wild flowers and bird song, heady with the scent of honeysuckle and alive with the drone of bees and insects – a veritable store house for my natural history collection.

It was also a place that became, like so many in Devon and Cornwall, both a natural playground and a schoolroom as my juvenile curiosity in the countryside steadily, and unconsciously, grew into a lasting fascination. They were perfect days. Like all childhood memories. I remember only that the sun always shone, and that Mrs Brown left me to run wild through the fields and lanes, discovering birds' nests and butterflies, marvelling at the delicate industry of spiders, and revelling in the freedom of being allowed to discover and enjoy the countryside by myself, bringing home many delights for my nature table.

The people of Delabole even spoke a different language. When Brown (he was always called Brown, hardly ever Henry) asked me, 'Where be gwain, maid – gwain bayd?' or 'Be' ee' avin a dish' o tay?' I just stared at him – speechless. It was two summers before I could understand every word and realised he was asking, 'Where are you going, girl – to bed?' and 'Would you like a cup of tea?' and another year before I could answer in his own broad dialect.

The quarry is like a deep white bowl

The North Devon Coastal Path

Whenever I've walked along the craggy clifftops of the North Devon coastal path, especially on the stretch from Hartland Point to Morwenstow, my eyes have been drawn – like most people's are, I'm sure – to the big empty sky, the endless expanse of the ocean, and the fabulous formation of cliffs and rocks that make this coastline so spectacular.

I had no idea, however, that while I was busy taking in this vast panorama, one of Nature's most marvellous processes was taking place immediately beneath my feet ; a creation that was just as spectacular – but almost invisible.

These clifftops were once the home of Britain's rarest butterfly, the Large Blue, which was officially declared extinct in 1981. Its survival depended on a carefully balanced habitat where sheep cropped the grass and this enabled colonies of ants to survive. These ants took the eggs of the Large Blue butterfly underground to their tunnels, mistaking them for their own eggs. As the caterpillars developed, they lived off the colony of ants, and eventually emerged as perfect blue butterflies. This must surely have been one of Nature's most wonderful tricks. But the balance was upset, and the Large Blue butterfly has now sadly disappeared.

It is tragic that, walking along this lovely coastal path, one can no longer see a flash of blue fluttering among the yellow of gorse or purple of heather. If you do, you can be sure you'll have seen a little miracle.

When you drive across the roof of Exmoor along the A39 over the Somerset/Devon border, the road offers tantalising glimpses of the sea framed against a landscape of deep valleys and splendid hills. All along this coastline the farmland runs rich and full to the very edge of the cliffs. At harvest time, when the days grow short and the sky fills with heavy clouds from the Atlantic, the combines and tractors often look as if they're defying gravity as they disappear over the slope of a field, and hang, almost suspended, between land and sea.

In the summertime the visitor sees only the beautiful face of this coastline. In winter it can be wild and savage. Dozens of ships have come to grief here, and scores of men have lost their lives in the wild Atlantic waves. From Lynton down to Bude every village has its own legacy of shipwreck and heroism at sea, and even on the calmest, most sparkling day, the lighthouse is a poignant reminder that the sea and the cliffs aren't always so hospitable. Hartland Point itself is fenced off, but one can visit the little white lighthouse which lies almost hidden at the foot of the cliffs.

The rocks and cliffs around Hartland Point are perhaps the most exciting on the whole north coast of Devon and Cornwall. It is not their height that is so dramatic as their shapes which are so fascinating. I find that I can look at those cliffs for hours on end, forming strange creatures out of the rock face.

The stout wall of Clovelly harbour has made this a safe haven for small fishing boats for more than three hundred years, but it is the quaintness of the town's steep cobbled streets that attracts most visitors nowadays.

At the village of Stoke, just below Hartland Point, the tower of St Nectan's church stands proud above the landscape. As one of the tallest in Devon, it can be seen for many miles. The rood-screen inside the church is very fine.

At Morwenstow you'll find one of the most beautiful little churches along this coastline. In the mid nineteenth century its vicar, the Rev. R. S. Hawker, built a small hut on the cliffside from flotsam and jetsam gleaned off the beach. He was nicknamed the Mad Vicar of Morwenstow, for he spent much of his time living in the hut and writing poetry. But his words show that he wasn't mad – just a dreamer. And surrounded by such beauty, who can blame him?

Appledore and Instow

There are many attractive narrow streets in the villages of Devon and Cornwall, but there can be none so pretty as those which slope straight down to Appledore's quay. The cottages which line the streets are mostly Georgian, with typical flat fronts, and the inhabitants keep them painted in a variety of pretty pastel colours.

The men of the village were never more than one narrow cobbled street away from the sea where their boats lay at anchor – a forest of masts growing out of the mud of the rivers Taw and Torridge at low tide.

Although the bar at the mouth of the estuaries is notorious, sailing is very popular here.

No one can say exactly when Appledore became a centre for shipbuilding. One of the earliest records refers to a vessel of 250 tons being launched there in 1568, and certainly by the mid-eighteenth century at least five brigantines and schooners were being launched every year.

In 1968, just two hundred and eighty years after it was first built, a replica of the Hudson's Bay Company's first ship, the Nonsuch, *was built by a local firm, Hinks & Son.*

There are still several independent boatbuilders scattered all along the coastline, but the pride of Appledore shipbuilders can be found at Bidna March, the site of the largest covered shipyard in Europe.

Apart from shipbuilding and fishing, smuggling was an important part of the livelihood of this small Devon town until about a century ago.

The beach at Instow stretches in a slim, pale golden line for almost as far as the eye can see – and when you're six that's an awful long way. I spent two glorious weeks on this beach in 1951, and sampled my first holiday in a caravan. It was a large, bottle-green metal box parked at the far end of a field, which it shared with other, smaller vans and a flock of sheep.

Every evening the sheep would gather at our end of the field and jostle for a sheltered spot under the van, banging into the galvanised bath that was slung under the floor. The bumping and clanging was a nightly ritual, and no human ever got to sleep until all the sheep were quite comfortable.

I loved to watch the little boats which were moored in the estuary. At high tide, they would bob around their buoys but when the tide went out, they would lean gently towards the mud.

Villages of Mid-Devon

The compact market town of Hatherleigh has always been
something of a crossroads for me on my drives through Devon. It
straddles the road halfway between Tavistock and Bideford, its
houses and shops precariously balanced on the edge of the steep
hill that twists and turns its way down through the cattle market,
past the old coaching house and a blaze of colourful flower boxes
and tubs.

Look at any map of the area and you'll see that the town is
surrounded by a tracery of narrow Devon lanes, with a tiny
village or hamlet at every other crossroads or junction, tucked
away behind lush Devon hedgerows, or slumbering in the hollow
of a small river valley. It's a landscape unlike any other in the
county, and well worth leaving the main roads to explore and
enjoy at leisure. Bishops Nympton, just outside South Molton, is
a typical village.

Exmoor and Doone Country

One of the nicest things about riding is that I've been able to enjoy so many secret places – like the lovely Hoccombe Water on Exmoor where the hills dip and fold in a series of gentle curves following the busy stream until it joins Badgworthy Water. This is Doone Country, the corner of Exmoor immortalised by R. D. Blackmore in his novel, Lorna Doone.

My four-footed companion on a recent ride there was a retired stag hunter and he knew the country well, picking his way with expert care between the rocky outcrops before we strode over the turf of Lank Combe, described by Blackmore as being 'carved out of the mountains in a perfect oval'.

I'd been chasing the ghosts of Lorna Doone and John Ridd. But they have long since gone, leaving the sky and the moors to me and my old hunter.

My ride through Doone Country was a pleasant way to spend a sunny autumnal Saturday afternoon, and a good excuse to get to know another corner of Exmoor.

But for many people the area is almost one of pilgrimage. Blackmore's novel has filled their minds with so many images they come to see for themselves the site of Carver Doone's home in the Exmoor hills, to follow Badgworthy Water through its wooded valley and discover the spot where young John Ridd first saw, and fell in love with the heroine Lorna Doone on St Valentine's day in 1675. And no visit to Doone Country would be complete without a peep inside Oare Church where Carver shot Lorna on her wedding day.

South Molton

I got to know South Molton quite well on my many trips to North Devon. It's an attractive market town always bustling with people and cars surrounded by a network of river valleys and good farmland.

But I think I saw it at its best at ten o'clock on a frosty winter's evening when the whole place was deserted. I'd motored down from London and needed somewhere to stay before driving on to a filming location early the next morning. As I drove up and down the main street, around the empty square, and manoeuvred through the narrow side roads, it could almost have been 1881 – not 1981. The iron balcony on the Medical Hall looked fine and delicate in the beam of my headlights, and the Victorian and Georgian buildings seemed to sit more comfortably in their surroundings without the usual crush of cars and other modern noises.

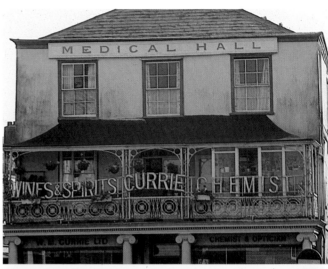

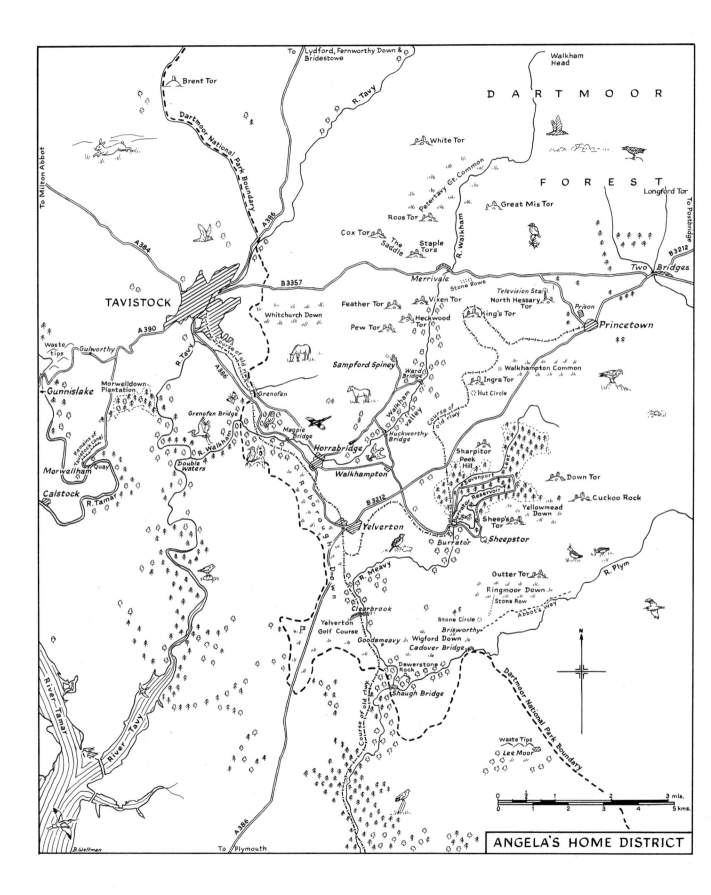

ANGELA'S HOME DISTRICT

Walkham Valley

As an end to one of the BBC's *In the Country* series, the producer, Peter Crawford, devised a show called 'Winter Reflections', in which all the regular contributors presented a profile of their favouite part of the country. I, obviously, chose Dartmoor, and specifically the stretch of river that runs through the Walkham Valley just below our house.

Some weeks after the programme, I received a letter from two viewers saying how much they'd enjoyed the programme, and how clever I was to disguise my favourite riverside walk by using the pseudonym, River Walkham. They knew the area quite well, they said, having holidayed there for several years, but had never come across the name Walkham – which just goes to show how lucky I am to live in such a carefully protected, relatively unknown part of the countryside. For the Walkham is not a pseudonym; it's very real, and one of the loveliest river valleys in Devon.

When Chris and I first found our house over thirteen years ago, we had no idea that the river was so close to the bottom of our garden. The thickly-wooded banks running steeply down from the fence effectively concealed both the sight and the sound of the water. What we saw first, after the jungle of garden and simple charm of the old stone house, was a cloud of bluebells swamping the wood with colour. It was only after we'd wandered through the trees and around the edge of the blue and green carpet, that we caught sight of the water sparkling and chasing through the trees. We'd already fallen for the house and the garden, but the sight of the river and the cool green of the wood convinced us that this was where we wanted to put down our roots.

Since the day we arrived in 1969, I've walked with the

The River Walkham, one of the loveliest rivers in Devon, with Grenofen Bridge in the background

dogs through some part of that wood and along a stretch of the river bank on almost every day that I've been at home. The dogs love the wild chases through crunchy dead leaves and squelchy mud after a rabbit or squirrel scent, leaving me to soak up the clear air, and the simple loveliness of everything around.

The river springs to life thirteen miles to the north, 1800 feet above sea level in a soggy peat bog at Walkham Head. From there it scurries and scampers over granite boulders and shingle beds towards the aptly named junction at Double Waters, a mile below our house, where it join forces with the Tavy to flow into the Tamar, and eventually into Plymouth Sound.

There's nothing lazy about the progress it makes seaward, forever rushing and tumbling over itself as if it cannot reach its destination fast enough, hurtling along at breakneck speed and living up to its reputation of being one of the fastest-flowing waterways in Devon. Before reaching us, the river has washed over the salmon spawning beds above Ward Bridge, gurgled cheekily past the attractive riverside hamlet at Huck-worthy, skidded over the weir and under the ancient bridge at Horrabridge, and tickled the toes of visitors at the beauty spot at Magpie Bridge. It comes to us a seasoned traveller – anxious to rush on to its next milestone at Grenofen Bridge, too busy to stop and admire the valley.

The big advantage of all this speed is that the river never has a chance to get dirty, or 'mankey'. The river bed and banks are always clear of rubbish, and the water stays crystal clear. The main disadvantage is that it is constantly changing the shape of the river. When Chris and I first saw the Walkham it was a narrow, bendy sliver of water that bounced around tree trunks like a child on a fairground helterskelter. But winter floods and the relentless scouring of the water have undermined the banks, swept away mature trees, and carved a wider, straighter path. This winter, a whole row of trees have suddenly had their roots exposed, and we know it's only a

Double Waters, where the Walkham joins the Tavy

question of time and high floods before they, too, are swept downstream.

This combination of an ancient wood and running water provides a marvellously varied habitat for a veritable catalogue of birds and mammals, insects and plants.

In the summer, hardly a day goes by without the buzzards mewing and calling on the thermals, and I'm sure the woodpeckers must give themselves a headache with all the hammering that goes on. Whenever we go through the gate from the bottom of the garden into the woods, you can be sure that the first sound we hear, after the initial whooping and yelping of the dogs, is the agitated screech of the busybody blackbird warning everything in the wood of approaching danger – as if the dogs hadn't done that already!

The old weathered oaks and beeches are alive with every conceivable woodland bird. Most of them like the finches and tits, the wagtails, nuthatches and jays come out of the trees to feed in the garden alongside the thrushes and robins. So once in the wood, I look out for the shyer visitors who shun our hospitality, like long-tailed tits and the diminutive siskin which I hear more often than I see. Just occasionally I'll catch the iridescent flash of a kingfisher skimming above the water, and am always delighted by the antics of the little white-throated dipper who curtsies and bows on the midstream boulders, then defies all the laws of nature by walking under water!

In our first year at Grenofen, we were thrilled to find a pair of herons making occasional forays up-river and flying over the house. Now these huge birds have bred and increased so successfully that I'm almost guaranteed to see at least one on every walk. They're such graceful birds when they're caught standing in the water, motionless and poised, ready to strike at their prey. But they look perfectly ridiculous and thoroughly uncomfortable roosting in trees, and I've ruffled their dignity more than once by laughing out loud at them – especially when they sit, four at a time, in a tree just below our garden.

When the gorse is in bloom, and the brambles are covered in starbursts of white flowers, the grassy banks of the river are alive with the rainbow colours of dragonflies and butterflies. In my sitting-room, I have a delicate water-colour depicting a pair of female Brown Hairstreaks – one of the rare butterflies found in the valley – feasting on oak and blackthorn. It was painted by Robin Armstrong, one of the most talented young painters I've met, who also happens to be our local water bailiff.

The river running under Grenofen and Huckworthy bridges

He's fashioned in the mould of a true countryman, applying his skills in fieldcraft to guarding his salmon and catching poachers as expertly as he does to breathing life into his countryside paintings. Although I reckon to know my river fairly well, to walk along the bank with someone like Robin, is to see it with fresh eyes. Many of his paintings feature the brightly-coloured, curiously-shaped toadstools and fungi that abound in the wood. I'd never really taken much notice of them until I started spotting them in his work, and now I've become something of a convert, searching out the magpie ink cap or photographing in detail the amazing colours and forms of the tree fungi which sprout like multi-petticoated crinolines from the stumps of dead or dying wood.

I can't get as excited about mosses and lichens, but knowledgeable friends tell me that our wood is a collectors' paradise. The plants love the damp atmosphere in the valley, and in the winter it looks like a primeval forest: every oak is decked out in green velvet, with individual trees becoming a microcosm of plant life as several species colonise each of the branches. The colours range from rich bottle-green to the palest hue of a fragile new leaf, and manage to over-ride the dank brown of dead leaves, or the bare branches of slumbering trees. Even on the dullest, most dreary winter's day, the wood can look almost fresh and springlike.

We have foxes, of course. There's an earth very close to the garden, so I often catch sight of the adults sneaking home at dawn and, in the summer, the vixen competes with our resident owl for dominance of the night air-waves. It's an eerie combination, the screech of the bird, the half-scream, half-bark of the fox – no wonder some people think the moor is haunted!

When we were buying the house, we asked a builder-friend to survey the property for us, and then suggest a realistic buying price. I remember he sat with us in the estate agent's office telling him all the things that were wrong with the house. It had woodworm and damp, needed a new roof and total renovation. In fact, in his opinion, we'd do better to pull it down and start again. However, he knew we wanted the house, so eventually he came to the crunch – the price. He mentioned a figure that was way below the asking price, but added magnanimously, 'We'll give you two hundred for the view.'

I often recall that moment when I look out from one of the windows onto the fields and woodland around us, all bursting with life, or watch the trees turn from summer green to fiery autumn gold, then sparkle under a cloak of winter snow. Having lived here for thirteen years, I know it isn't worth two hundred pounds at all – it's priceless.

A Cathedral Road

Whenever I drive through the countryside of my home county, I never fail to give thanks to the man who invented Devon 'hedges'. They're built of natural stone and mortared together with earth so that a mature wall grows and develops like a tenement block with snails and spiders, field mice and voles living cheek by jowl with wrens and robins, while the bare earth is colonised by pennywort, honeysuckle, the stately spikes of fox-gloves, and primroses that cluster together like bowls of clotted cream.

All this should more than satisfy those people who, like me, despair of wire fences. But the Devon hedge has even more to offer – in the trees and bushes that grow from their tops. There's blackthorn and beech, oak and hazel – all trimmed and laid with care and skill to create a thick stock-proof fence, and a thing of beauty. I'm always saddened when I drive through those parts of the country where hedges have been grubbed out to create massive prairie-like fields in which half a dozen combines can work simultaneously. I'm sure it's more profitable for the farmers but it's robbed the countryside of a valuable asset.

I'm glad that Devon is known for its sheep and cattle rather than its corn and wheat, for it's meant that we've kept our heritage of small fields, and the wealth of trees and hedges that divide them – especially the trees which, in most of the older hedges, have been left to grow to full maturity and create the leafy lanes and wooded hillsides that are a feature of the West Country. Their graceful lines bring perspective and beauty to the landscape and, like the grandfather clock that reliably chimes every hour, they measure the passage of the year through spring buds and summer leaf, to autumn gold and winter's stark relief. Our countryside would be the poorer without them.

There's a road about ten miles or so to the north of our home which runs from Shortacombe to the village of Bridestowe across Fernworthy Down. A century or more ago, the road was lined with a Devon hedge and crop of beech trees. Over the years, a few of the trees were singled out and left to grow. Gradually, the hedge shrank back to form a fairly insignificant ridge, but the trees went on growing into what is now a masterpiece of natural architecture.

For a quarter of a mile, they stride along both sides of the road, each one a giant among trees. Their branches meet somewhere high above and, in summer especially, you get the feeling that you're passing under a vaulted roof supported by corinthian pillars. When I first drove down this road, I was so struck by the unexpected grandeur of it, that I had to pull in to the verge and get out of the car to make sure my eyes hadn't deceived me. Later that night, as I drove back along the same stretch of road, the trees were floodlit in my headlights and the effect was even more cathedral-like.

I often travel that way now since the road leads to a favourite restaurant, and the riding centre at Bridestowe where my horse Kate and I do battle with the disciplines of dressage. But familiarity hasn't bred contempt. I'm still slightly in awe of those mighty beech trees, and always slow down when I pass them to make the picture last a little longer. And when I finally turn onto the main road, leaving the avenue behind, I often reflect that while the human race undoubtedly produced some very clever and talented men, Nature is still the undisputed Master Builder.

In summer, this road will be a long green tunnel

Sampford Spiney

William Crossing, who was undoubtedly one of the greatest writers ever to chronicle the history and landscape of Dartmoor, wrote in his famous *Guide to Dartmoor* that 'Sampford Spiney hardly deserves the name of a village, consisting as it does only of a church, a school and ancient manor house and a few dwellings.' But a 'village' it is, and one of the most attractive, secret places on the southern moor.

It straddles a loop of land that gives access to a few isolated homes and farms, above the Walkham Valley in the lee of Pew Tor. Unless you were to actually make for Sampford Spiney as a point on the map, the chances of driving through it by accident are rare.

I first 'discovered' it on one of my daily rides more than eight years ago. I'd often seen signposts pointing to the village, but had never bothered to go out of my way to see what lay at the end of the lane. But on a horse, any lane or by-way that offers a change of scene is too good to resist, so I rode into town, one autumn morning, and was immediately charmed by the timelessness of the place.

The three main buildings are grouped around a natural sloping village green that's strewn with boulders and sliced in two by a fresh moorland spring. The manor house, once lived in by Tudor relatives of the local hero, Sir Francis Drake, is now a farmhouse but it's been maintained and restored with care and an eye for history, so it still has all the charm and grace that made it a fitting home for an Elizabethan lord of the manor.

The school house closed its doors to local children some years ago, and is now the home of an artist who plies between London, Venice and Sampford, capturing the essence of his three haunts in vibrant, living landscapes.

The centrepiece of this trio is undoubtedly the little church. No plain, country mouse this, tucked away in anonymity, but a pretty building with tall sparkling leaded windows, and a beautifully proportioned tower topped with decorative spires. It rests in the middle of a small churchyard, surrounded by a low Devon granite wall, and shaded by oak and beech.

It was once owned by those wealthy and much-travelled religious men of Plympton Priory – their coat of arms, two crossed keys, is carved in crisp lines above one of the south windows. When travelling from Plympton to Tavistock, the monks would stop to rest at Sampford before joining the ancient Abbot's Way into the town. Their journey was a testing one. It meant walking fifteen miles over bare, rugged moorland. In summer, the hardships were no doubt tempered by the sweet heather, the bird song and the clear open heavens. But in winter it must have been purgatory, making the warmth and respite of Sampford especially welcome.

Now that I've 'found' it, I often ride through the village. It's snug, and sheltered in its hiding place, well protected from the sharp winds that clip across the moor just a few hundred yards from its boundary. Nothing changes here, only the seasons. And if it weren't for the telegraph poles, you might almost believe when you stand on one corner of the green looking at the manor house and the church, that you'd stumbled upon a Brigadoon – a place where time has stood still for five hundred years and where Drake himself might beckon to you from the half-open door of the manor.

The church and manor house of Sampford Spiney

Tavistock, a Stannary town

I recently came across a reference to Tavistock in which the writer described the town as 'Devon at her sweetest and tenderest', and I don't think he was far wrong.

When Chris and I came to live on the outskirts of the town over thirteen years ago, we knew it only as a place to drive through on our way to North Devon. But since then, the small town with its Friday market and friendly shops has become a vital part of our lives and we have an affection for it which hasn't diminished over the years.

Scholars and historians are attracted here because of its antiquity. The Benedictine monks who owned Tavistock, built their beautiful Abbey on the banks of the river Tavy in 974. It was robbed and destroyed after the Dissolution of the monasteries nearly six hundred years later but small fragments have survived from which it is possible to trace the size and influence of the Abbey – like Betsy Grimball's Tower, and the graceful decorative medieval arches that were uncovered in the grounds of the parish church. They remind us not only of the power and wealth of those extraordinary men but also of their talent for building things of great beauty, and resilience.

Tavistock became an important centre for the wool trade in the fourteenth century, producing a coarse cloth known as 'Tavistocks'. And the great Tudor sea captain, Sir Francis Drake, was born and bred on a Tavistock farm.

But it's the legend that appears on the town's boundary markers that gives a clue to its most interesting period in history. The signs welcome you to 'Tavistock, an ancient Stannary Town', which means that for centuries it was one of only five towns in the county recognised as a centre for the tin trade. Later, when copper and arsenic, lead, wolfram and zinc were all dug out of the surrounding hills, Tavistock became a mining boom-town.

There are some wonderful descriptions of those times which have survived in newspapers and journals locked in the county archives. Imagine what it must have been like on a Saturday night in the late 1800s after the miners had collected their wages. It's said that they flocked to

'Tavistock, ancient Stannary Town' : the Tavy, Town Hall and the medieval parish church

the taverns in Tavistock in such numbers that the tiny streets were choked with their bodies standing shoulder to shoulder until you could walk on the heads of the miners. Perhaps it was someone trying to do just that who coined the saying that on a Saturday night 1½d. would buy you 'a pint of white ale and two black eyes'.

The men worked hard, and played hard, working in darkness, living in squalor, so the Saturday night booze-up was a short relief from lives that must have been mostly wretched and miserable. There were too many people, earning too little money (fourteen shillings a week was the average wage), crowded into too few houses. Contemporary writers claim that in the slum tenements of the town, the beds were never cold – as the night shift moved out, the day shift moved in, and only on Saturday nights could the fleas go down to the Tavy to wash! The slums have gone, and only on Tavistock Goosy Fair day in October are the streets now crowded fit to burst. Then the main square becomes a fairground filled with cheap-jacks and bargains, and the carnival spirit rules from dawn till dusk.

But there are a few more permanent reminders of that extraordinary era. For example, John Taylor's master-piece of engineering, the Tavistock Canal, still begins its lugubrious journey to Morwellham from the anony-mous commercial wharves and warehouses tucked away

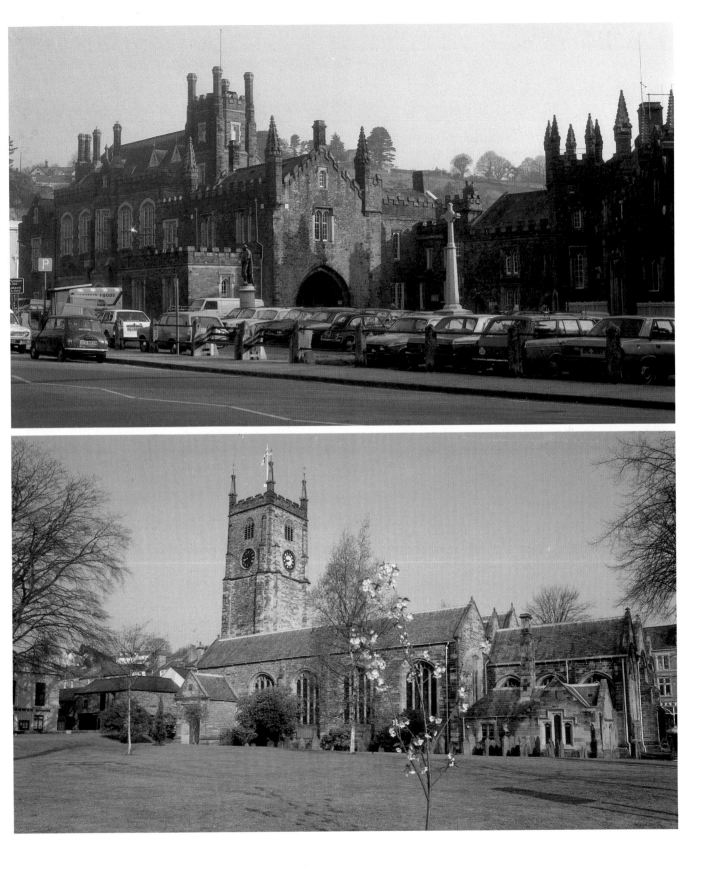

behind the main Plymouth road; the cottages built by the Duke of Bedford to ease the housing shortage of the 1860s still accommodate Tavistock families, and Tavistock Square is dominated by the dignified civic buildings that were financed by the Duke of Bedford with some of his profits from the Devon Great Consols Mine.

A friend recently showed me an old postcard of the town illustrating the square and parish church in 1860. There were crinolines where you'd now find jeans, and a wagon instead of lorries – but apart from that, the picture could almost have been taken yesterday.

And that's what I love about Tavistock. Like so many of our British towns, it's found its own pace in life, refusing to be bullied along on a wave of change for change's sake. Tavistock reminds me of an old wise woman sitting with arms folded on the banks of the Tavy, sheltered by the Dartmoor hills, and saying, 'I've been here for centuries, and I'm not moving.' It makes it a very reassuring place to live.

The redundant railway viaduct, and the Bedford Cottages built in the 1860s; Tavistock's Friday market

It's a fine old market town where you can buy anything from a tin tack to a tractor, and which boasts one of the best old-fashioned grocer's shops in Devon. On market day, the stalls are piled with local produce – honey and cream, fresh eggs, butter and chicken as well as flowers, fruit and vegetables. It bustles without rushing, has pace without panic.

There are dozens of antique and curio shops tucked away in quiet squares and around twisty corners, and it's a joy to shop in a place where most customers are known by name, and personal service is given willingly with a smile, not grudgingly with a scowl. Whenever people ask, 'Where do you live?' and I reply, 'near Tavistock', I am no longer surprised when those who know the area come out with the same response: 'Oh yes,' they say with a smile, 'we know Tavistock – it's such a *nice* little town.'

Morwellham

One of the great bonuses of a job like mine is that I meet so many really nice people. Some are household names, both national and international; others have probably never been heard of outside their small, tight community. Jack Adams was such a man. A water bailiff by profession, he was also a storyteller and countryman, and the main love of his working life flowed unhurriedly past the bottom of his garden – the River Tamar.

Jack lived in the village of Morwellham, a place I'd never visited until the morning I went to interview him about his work on the river. If you look at a map of the Tavistock area, you'll see that Morwellham is at the end of a single-track road on a knuckle of land formed by the twist and swing of the river. You don't pass through Morwellham, or casually drop in on your way to somewhere else. You either go there intentionally – or not at all. So it had been a blank on my map, and frankly I had no idea what I was going to find when I arrived.

The route was well signposted from the Tavistock road, and followed a straight flat unerring line past Morwelldown Plantation and good Devon farmland. Then the road began to drop downhill. Gradually at

Jack Adams' cottage, and Morwellham Quay which lies on a knuckle of land formed by the twist and swing of the River Tamar

first, curling left then right, and suddenly tumbling headlong through the trees, steep and impatient to reach the bottom. A Methodist chapel loomed up on the left, a cluster of houses followed the sweep of the road around to the right, and then the tarmac came to an end. I was in a small square of granite and slate-hung buildings. A hundred yards away, smoke curled from the neat row of chimneys above a line of semi-detached cottages, and straight ahead lay the path to Jack's cottage.

It was a tiny, slate-covered building encased in a sparkling white picket fence. The ground in front of the cottage was as flat and wide as three tennis courts, edged by the river which made a steady dignified progress past mud banks and reeds.

We talked about his work as a bailiff, of keeping one jump ahead of the poachers, protecting the fish, enjoying the peace and tranquillity of the river, sharing it with herons and kingfishers, always looking for the elusive, shadowy figure of the otter.

Jack loved his river, and it shone through every word he spoke. We were standing on the bank looking over the water which ran thick and muddy that day, after almost a week of heavy rain, with reeds and twigs floating on the surface as they navigated a lazy path downstream. I suddenly noticed what Jack was leaning on. It looked like a sturdy granite bollard, the sort you'd expect to see around the dockside at Falmouth or Plymouth, but not several miles inland on the muddy banks of the Tamar.

'That's a bit grand for your little rowing boat, isn't it?' I asked. He smiled. 'Come with me,' he said, 'I have a photograph I think you'll find interesting.'

In the snug, cosy parlour where Mrs Adams had laid tea and biscuits, Jack pointed to a photograph on the wall. It was of Morwellham in 1868 and showed quite clearly the hill I'd driven down, the row of neat cottages, the Methodist chapel and cluster of houses, even Jack's own cottage which could be seen slap in the middle.

Morwellham Quay c. 1868, showing the pair of schooners moored in the huge dock (photo. Morwellham Quay Museum)

But what dominated the photograph was a pair of elegant schooners moored in a huge dock that cut into the flat plane in front of the cottage. The ships were surrounded by piles of ore waiting to be loaded on board, and the whole place was circled by an overhead railway. I had come to a village which I had taken to be a quite insignificant Devon backwater, but the photograph in my hands showed that Morwellham had once been a major inland commercial port. The contrast was startling. We went back out into the garden, and while I drank tea, Jack brought the history of Morwellham to life.

It had been a port since the beginning of the twelfth century when roads over Dartmoor to Tavistock and Launceston were nothing more than muddy tracks and it could take a day or more to bring goods overland from Plymouth. But a boat could navigate the Tamar from Plymouth Sound to Morwellham in two hours, leaving just a four-mile trek inland to be completed by packhorse.

Cider for the monks at Tavistock Abbey, and sea sand for farmers to lime their fields passed regularly through the tiny port for centuries. When manganese, lead and copper were found in the hills around Tavistock and Gunnislake towards the end of the eighteenth century, Morwellham grew in size and importance.

A canal which took fourteen years to build brought iron barges laden with ore from the centre of Tavistock to the slopes above the village from where the cargo was trundled down on a railway to the quayside. Then in 1844, the richest copper deposits in Europe were discovered at Blanchdown on the hills above Gunnislake. The Devon Great Consols Mine became the biggest, wealthiest, most important commercial influence in the area, changing the face of Tavistock, Gunnislake and the whole of the Tamar Valley, including Morwellham.

The Dartington Trust took over Morwellham in 1970 and have begun reconstructing some of its major features

The mining company built their own railway from Blanchdown to Morwellham to carry the ore, defeating the final sharp drop into the village with a mighty planed incline which shot down the hillside, and delivered the trucks on the quay. A new dock was built, two hundred and ninety feet long, sixty foot wide and sixteen foot deep, large enough to berth six vessels of three hundred tons each, while the flat ground from the water's edge was tiled over so that none of the precious ore would be wasted.

When the supply of copper started to decline, arsenic took its place, to be shipped mostly to America to protect the cotton crops from the devastating effects of the boll weevil.

While Jack spoke, he employed the infinite skill of the classic storyteller, using words like bricks to build images and scenes that came to life all around us. It was easy to see the tall masts of the sailing ships weave their way between the trees overhanging the river bank, to hear the clank and clatter of the cooperage where the ore casks were fashioned, the swoosh and creak of mighty waterwheels, mingling with the rumble of trolleys on the railway, the din and racket of dockers loading and unloading vessels, and see the lanes crowded with the captains and sailors who swaggered to the Ship Inn with tales of voyages to America, the Baltic and the major ports of Europe.

Ships arrived bringing timber and coal for the mines, salt and sea sand for the farmers, and general goods for the local communities, then left carrying the rich proceeds of Devon Great Consols and its neighbours.

The whistle of the first train on the newly-opened Great Western Railway line from Plymouth to Tavistock in 1859 sounded the death knell for Morwellham. The journey by river had been swift, but the railway was even faster, and by the end of the century it had taken all the trade away from the Tamar port. The village that had been one of the most important ports of its kind in Europe, that had handled 750,000 tons of copper ore and 72,000 tons of arsenic worth over three and a half million pounds from just one mine, and had been a vital link in trade and communications for almost a thousand years, sank back into sleepy obscurity. The Tavistock Canal is now lined with pampas and beech and forms an attractive centrepiece for that town's municipal park at the start of its $4\frac{1}{2}$-mile course, while at the far end, above Morwellham, it's been diverted to provide power for a hydro-electric generating station.

The railway and great incline were dismantled, the great dock and the river itself had silted up and grown over, leaving the vast tiled floors of the quay to be slowly and effectively covered by the turf. For those with eyes to see, there were still the remains of the kilns, a few yards of uncovered tiles, and the incongruous bollards beside a cut in the river which, on closer inspection, looked just a little too straight to be anything other than man-made. But, as with so many bits of history, if you don't know what you're supposed to be looking for, they're meaningless. Without Jack's potted history, the ghosts of Morwellham would have hung in the tree tops with the wind and the birds, but he brought the place to life for me, and kindled an interest in the history of mining in the Tamar Valley that was to have far-reaching effects – but that's another story!

In 1970, The Dartington Trust took over Morwellham and began reconstructing some of its major features, so that visitors today can see almost exactly what the place would have looked like at its zenith. When Jack Adams died a few years ago, his widow moved to another village, and sold their cottage to the Trust who are now refurbishing it with furniture and artefacts from the 1870s to give visitors some idea of what it was like to live and work in the community a hundred years ago.

Although people won't hear again as I did Jack Adams' colourful, vivid description of the village, his home is about to play its own role in re-telling the Morwellham story. And considering what a great storyteller Jack was, I think he'd appreciate that.

An aerial view showing the restoration of Morwellham Quay, taken in 1981 (photo. Western Morning News)

The Mine of Mines

When you drive from Tavistock towards Gunnislake, down the steep hill from Gulworthy towards the Tamar Valley, you can't miss the great stain of barren earth and waste tips that spreads over the hills to your right like a giant canker on the land. Surrounded by lush green fields where sheep and cows fatten, and where the gentle industry of market gardening is practised, that scar is all that's left to remind us that an area now famous for the quality of its strawberries and tomatoes was once the home of the richest copper mine in Europe – the Devon Great Consols.

Not long after my trip to Morwellham, when my appetite for the history of the valley had been whetted by Jack Adams, I met two amateur industrial archaeologists, Joan and Terry Doyle, who ran mini-safari tours with a difference – they visited the major eighteenth- and nineteenth-century industrial sites in the Tamar Valley, introducing people like me to a slice of history that we'd never even considered.

We walked over piles of rubble, and ivy-covered ruins that had once been the site of the Tamar Firebrick and Tile Works on Hingston Down from where tiles and decorative bricks had been exported to Russia. We peered down into narrow shafts where waterwheels had sucked and slurped, providing power for a whole host of machines. On Kit Hill, we stood a thousand feet above sea level by a memorial to the valley's long-dead miners, looking down across the valley to the sparkling strip of water that threads its way into Plymouth Sound, and marvelled that men should have traded a life in the clean sweet air, for the dark dank underground tunnels of the silver, lead, copper and arsenic mines. On the banks of the Tamar, we re-created in our mind's eye the days when this lovely waterway was both county boundary and a main commercial highway, with pleasure steamers and merchant ships plying the upper stretches of the river beyond the graceful arches of Calstock viaduct, on their way to Morwellham, the busiest copper port in Queen Victoria's empire.

And then there was Devon Great Consols, the 'mine of mines' that had reshaped the landscape, and the lives of the entire district. Engineers had suspected for some years that the area known as Blanchdown was rich in copper, but the 6th Duke of Bedford, who owned the land, wasn't prepared to give up what were his finest pheasant coverts to a gang of miners. His successor, the seventh duke, was more practically-minded – and financially motivated. So in return for a commission worth one-twelfth of all the ore extracted, he signed over the site for twenty-one years in March 1844. That single stroke of the pen robbed him of the best shooting rights on his estate, but earned him £250,000 in royalties, some of which he ploughed back into the area by building two hundred and fifty cottages, the attractive covered market and the town hall and magistrates' court which border the suitably-named Bedford Square in Tavistock. The houses, incidentally always known as Bedford Cottages, were built for just £22 each, and these days change hands for around £18,000!

When the mine was at the height of its prosperity, it covered one hundred and forty acres, had twelve main shafts, with forty-five miles of underground levels. There were thirty-three waterwheels turning on steady, measured strokes night and day, non-stop throughout the year. There were foundries where they made their own steam engines and railway locomotives. Pumping houses and engine shafts, coopers and rope-makers, blacksmiths and boilermakers. More than a thousand people worked in the mine, and five thousand more were supported by ancillary industries.

In 1870, when the copper started to run thin, the mine turned to arsenic production, by hacking out the rich deadly ore which lay alongside the old copper lodes. Apart from its use as a pesticide against the boll weevil in America, it was also used in the manufacturing of glass and enamel, paints and dyes and, of course, as a poison.

The ore was ground to a light gravel, then roasted to produce a thick pungent yellow vapour which was fed through a series of flues and a labyrinth where the vapour condensed on tile walls, to be scraped off as

The site of what was the richest copper mine in Europe

rough arsenic crystals. They were put through the process again, and the result was a fine white powder said to be 99.5% pure. It was believed that one-sixth of a teaspoon of arsenic from D.G.C. was enough to kill a man, and that the mine held enough ore to poison the whole world.

The crystals needed to be scraped off the labyrinth walls by hand, and the men employed to do the work had to bind their bodies and cover their faces against the deadly white crystals. But it's said that no cut on their bodies ever healed while they worked in the flues, and the dust crept into their pores so that at night their skins glowed in the dark with a green phosphorescence, like creatures from another planet.

For fifty-seven years, the mine dominated the valley. Shares that had cost £1 in 1844 were changing hands at £800 each two years later, and although profits declined towards the end of the mine's life, every share earned £923 – a steady income of £44 11s a year. On Saturday 30 November 1901 all production at the mine ceased because of a petty boardroom row over finance and, since that time, no industry comparable in size, wealth or importance has ever replaced it in the Tavistock district.

I was so fascinated after my mini historical tour that I persuaded my employers, then Westward Television, to let me make a film about the valley and its extraordinary history. We called it *The Silent Valley* since, compared to the days when the Tamar Valley had been a noisy, booming, industrial heartland, that's exactly what it was.

Most of the film was shot amongst the ruined engine-houses and mine workings in the valley, with archive material from the wonderful collection of the Truro County Library. But during our research, we came across a group of young pot-holers who had explored the underground levels at Devon Great Consols, and were prepared to re-enact a mining sequence for us – underground.

A chimney-stack from the old arsenic works

It took weeks to get clearance for the project but, eventually, one overcast Sunday morning we all assembled outside a small hole in the rock face at the site of an old entrance to the shaft named Wheal Maria. We must have looked a motley bunch. Apart from the director and film crew, there were a dozen or so cavers. We were dressed in boiler suits and climbing boots and each wore a tin helmet with a miner's lamp attached. The cavers lowered the film equipment into the mine first, then one by one we followed them and began the journey underground.

The hole in the rock led through a short, low tunnel to a ledge above a sixty-foot drop. As I crawled along on all fours to the edge of the tunnel, I could see the cluster of lights way below that located the position of the climbers who'd already made the descent. In the light of their torches, the flimsy rope and aluminium climbing-ladder that dangled down into the black bottomless-looking space seemed very narrow and insecure. But that was the only way down – and there was no turning back now.

Ghosts of the past : remains of an old engine-house

I took my courage, and the ladder, in both hands, swung out from the security of the ledge, hooked my left foot in one of the rungs, and slowly climbed down, followed by the rest of the crew. As we crowded together at the bottom of the pit, the light from our helmets made our surroundings look quite bright, but a glance along the pitch black tunnels made it clear that this was only an illusion, and we were in no place to go wandering off alone to explore. The cavers had done a good underground 'recce' and took us straight to a cavernous stope – or chamber – where several miners would have worked together, hacking ore from the face.

Our 'actors' were dressed shabbily, given soft felt hats like those the old miners would have worn, onto which they stuck plain tallow candles, held in place with a handful of putty – the nearest we could get to the clay the men of the 1800s would have used. We wanted to illustrate not just the working conditions underground, but the dangers that faced the men from explosions, rock falls, and fatigue – for many men were killed by falling from the long, perpendicular ladders on their climb out of the mines at the end of a ten-hour shift.

While the various sequences were being rehearsed, and filmed, there was little for me to do, and one of the non-acting cavers offered to give me a tour of the more accessible underground passages. So half a dozen of us went deeper into the workings, along one of the long narrow corridors that ran off the main chamber. We walked in single file – there was no room to do anything else as the walls brushed our shoulders and the roof was just a few inches above our helmets. If I suffered from claustrophobia, now was not the time to find out.

Straight ahead lay nothing but a great black void. Only the small area directly in front of me was lit by the lamp on my helmet and the spillover from the lamp in front. I was following shadows more than light. It was an eerie sensation, not helped by the fact that one of the power packs we each wore strapped around our waists had a fault, which made its wearer's light flicker and fail intermittently. I was very thankful indeed that it wasn't mine.

The roof and walls were dripping with stalactites that had fashioned themselves into fabulous designs of fairy castles and minarets, each shaded from yellow to deep orange by the copper ore still in the ground. The floor of the tunnel was flooded so we waded for over half a mile knee deep in copper-stained water. At last the tunnel opened up into another large underground 'cave'. The floor here was dry, and as we walked I could feel my toes squelching inside my waterlogged boots. The roof of the cave narrowed into a straight-sided shaft with wooden props squeezed between the walls, as if holding them apart. That was where men had worked – suspended above their colleagues, following the line of a copper lode or seam.

In the restricted light from our six small lamps, it was difficult to see more than a small section of the mine at one time, but the thing that immediately struck me was that here, a hundred feet below the surface, in this black sinister hole where I'd expected to find no colour at all, just depressing grey, the walls offered a technicoloured world of complete fantasy. It was a crystal cave where the ore sparkled and danced in the beams of our lamps, reflecting gold and white, orange and black. It was truly beautiful, and totally unexpected.

At the far end of the cave, a small rockfall had partially sealed the entrance to the next corridor, but we scrambled over the top and dropped down into a wider more airy corridor than the last and walked just a few hundred yards to our goal – the main shaft that connected three floors of underground workings. The walls here were timber-lined and, looking at them, I could appreciate the description I'd read somewhere of underground tunnels being lined with timbers of such majestic proportions – some more than fifty foot long and two foot square – that they had the appearance of an aisle in a cathedral.

In truth, the shaft in which I was standing looked more like the lift hall at Harrods than the aisle of Exeter Cathedral but I could understand what they meant! At the centre of the shaft, there was a large, square hole – again wood-lined, which disappeared down into an uncertain void. We crowded around for a photograph to mark the occasion, with no one getting too close to the edge. Although the timber looked solid enough, it had been saturated by the constant drip of water from the walls, and in places you could push your finger through chunky beams as easily as a poker through butter.

We turned to retrace our steps and, on the walk back, I tried to imagine what it must have been like to work down there. It was hot and airless, and I was beginning to find it uncomfortable even though all I'd done was walk and sight-see for an hour or so. The miners had worked with the smoke of blasting, the choking dust from their own efforts with pick and shovel, burrowing like moles for ten hours a day. All for barely fourteen shillings a week, and only four days a year paid holiday. The images began crowding in – and none of them was very pleasant.

When we rejoined the main group, they'd finished filming and were ready to start the climb back to the surface. It was more difficult climbing up than it had been coming down. I hung in space feeling the ladder swing gently as I pulled myself hand over hand, boot over boot, back up the sixty-foot drop. It was arm-aching, and slightly nerve-wracking, especially the last few feet where we had to negotiate around a beam before we could scramble onto the safety of the ledge. But it took me only a few minutes, whereas the men who'd worked in the lowest levels of that black furnace had taken an hour to climb up to the sunlight – for there were no fancy extras like lifts in Wheal Maria.

We emerged from the tunnel weary and filthy, and sat on the grass breathing in great lungfuls of the clean, cool fresh air. Looking at our watches, we realised we'd been underground for more than five hours. We could hardly believe it, the time had gone so quickly, but it was well worth it. The scenes we'd filmed underground were superb and made a vital contribution to *The Silent Valley*.

On a personal note, the experience of standing in the bowels of the earth and summoning up the ghosts of the past, is one I shall never forget.

A Moorland Ride

When Roy Plomley asked me the inevitable question on *Desert Island Discs*, 'How would you cope with the loneliness?' I was able to answer without hesitation (and as much honesty as can be achieved in such a hypothetical situation), 'I'm a loner by nature, so I believe I would cope very well – in fact I think I'd quite enjoy it.'

Born an only child, I grew up accepting the need to be satisfied with my own company from time to time, and because I do such a public job in television, where every syllable and eye blink is under mass scrutiny, the contrast of solitude is a welcome relief. I think that's probably one of the main reasons why I feel completely at home on Dartmoor. I can surround myself with so much life and vitality, so many things to hold my attention and delight the eye, and yet still snatch a few moments' isolation. It's a perfect panacea, and when I tell people that it's my country existence of long walks and lonely rides that keeps me sane – I'm not kidding.

That doesn't mean I live the life of a hermit. Far from it. Although it's true that most of my riding on the moor is done with only the horse, and occasionally the dogs, for company, one of my favourite 'day treks' over a twelve-mile circular route, has been done in the company of friends who enjoy the scenery and freedom of the open moor as much as I do.

When my father was fifty-four and my mother fifty-two, they both plucked up enough courage to sit on a horse for the first time in their lives. A series of bad falls convinced Mother that she could appreciate horses better from the ground than in the saddle, but Father persevered and it became just like old times. Instead of the bicycles of my youth, we had horses, and set about discovering Dartmoor with the aid of a sturdy cob mare called Polly, a fine-limbed grey pony called Skippy, and a one-inch Ordnance Survey map.

The horses were hired to us every weekend from a stable just outside the village of Horrabridge, a location that gives access to miles of open moorland within just a few minutes. In the summer of 1975, we decided to

Dartmoor ponies shelter near the Burrator Reservoir

become a little more adventurous, and extend our two-hour Sunday morning forays to a ride that we knew would take most of the day, and cover some of the beauty spots we'd been visiting by car and on foot for many years.

We set out at about ten one Sunday morning, returning some hours later, having followed a route that I've taken many times since, and one that's become something of a 'bolt hole' when I need a complete day off – or just an excuse for doing nothing.

The first part of our journey took us through the leafy, wooded lanes above the Walkham Valley. Down the twisting hill to the granite arch of Ward Bridge, then steeply up past green fields and grazing sheep, to emerge breathless at the top of the hill, where tamed farmland gives way to wild moor, and the grey mangled bulk of Ingra Tor fills the sky.

Some of the tors on Dartmoor have fascinating peaks of weathered granite that make bold, sculptured outlines against the heavens. But others, like Ingra, manage to look more like a stonemason's scrap heap than a natural phenomenon. It was, no doubt, while looking at a tor just like this one that a Victorian lady traveller recorded in her journal: 'There are stones enough on Dartmoor to build all the cities of Europe, though I am almost afraid to mention it least the suggestion might be accepted.' Thank goodness no one did. Ingra may not be one of the most beautiful of spots on the moor but without it, and others like it, the moor would be a very bland, uninteresting place.

We rode over the crest of the hill, leaving the untidy sprawl of Ingra behind, and crossed the remains of the old railway line that used to run from Princetown, through Sheepstor village to Yelverton. On our left we could just make out the faint lines of an ancient hut circle and enclosure, the first of many we were to pass during the day. We took our bearing from the top of the next major landmark, Sharpitor, and headed towards it in a straight line, travelling almost due south, across the open ground. The moorland turf is coarse and lumpy here, strewn with boulders and scratchy tufts of gorse and heather. There are no marked bridleways or paths and yet, when we consulted the map, we found that by instinct we were riding along the track of one of the most ancient paths on the moor – a route taken by the monks of Plympton Priory on one of their many and varied journeys over Dartmoor to the faithful of the parishes in their care.

Immediately below Sharpitor, we hit the first of only two main roads that we'd be crossing that day. And as we waited for a gap in the weekend traffic that plied over the tarmac between Princetown and Yelverton, I was glad that we were out in the clean fresh air on horseback, and not stuck inside a family car. For the day was perfect. A few white clouds hung decoratively in the sky, and the light breeze was just cool and fresh enough to stop the sun burning into our faces and bare arms.

Most of the moorland sheep sat munching laconically in the scant shade of boulders and hawthorn, but a few were in groups by the side of the road, doggedly refusing to move while the cars whizzed by just inches from their noses. I'm told they do this because the smell of hot tarmac helps to keep the summer flies at bay. It could be that the teller was just pulling my leg, but it would explain why sheep have developed this suicidal habit when there's thousands of acres of open moorland available to them.

We kept the summit of Sharpitor on our left and rode across the slope of the hill towards the Forestry Commission's plantation of dark evergreens at Peek Hill. As we got closer to the top of the hill, the scene began to open up like the classic helicopter shots at the beginning of the film, *The Sound of Music*. If you remember, while Maria is singing away at the top of her voice, the camera gradually pulls away and the scene behind her grows and grows to reveal the magnificent sweep of the Austrian Alps. As we rode higher and higher up the ridge, the view from the other side of the hill slowly came up to meet us. First there was just the empty blue sky, then the bottom of the picture was

The River Walkham at Ward Bridge ; Ingra Tor

Remains of the old railway line; 'Dartmoor', the famous prison at Princetown; the Burrator Reservoir

pierced by the slender tips of conifers from the far hill, gradually swelling and growing into a vast plantation with the grey craggy top of Sheep's Tor looming up to the left.

And then suddenly the whole picture was filled with the flat silver calm of Burrator Reservoir. The valley had been flooded in the 1890s to provide water for the people of Plymouth and the sheet of water that now covers 119 acres is for me one of the finest man-made sights on the moor. There are those who object to flooding moorland valleys to provide reservoirs, but I must admit that I find it hard to support them when the end result is as stunningly beautiful as the one at Burrator.

Our view of the reservoir that summer's day, from the heights of Peek Hill, could not have been better. It was as flat as a mill pond, giving a perfect reflection of the trees that crowded around the water's edge, and a mirror for the sun, which looked in from time to time to powder her nose with a passing handful of cotton wool cloud.

We rode slowly down the hill, skirting the plantation and crossing part of the Devonport Leat, a granite-lined channel that was built to carry water from the high moor down into the town of Devonport – it was fashioned on Sir Francis Drake's famous leat, built two years earlier to carry water to Plymouth. Legend suggests that this was a magnanimous gesture by Drake to provide the people of Plymouth with the first supply of moorland water, but historians record, probably more accurately, that it was done to generate power at a group of mills he owned!

A narrow gravel path running from the east brought us out onto the road that circles the reservoir, so we turned left, heading for the far end of the lake, and the

One of the finest man-made sights on Dartmoor

path that would take us up through another fir plantation to the barren acres of Yellowmead Down. By now it
was almost noon and the Sunday morning drivers were
out in force heading for the picnic spots around the
reservoir. After half a mile, we were able to leave the
hollow clop of hooves on tarmac and make our way up
one of the rough paths that lace through the trees
leading to the moor.

The warmth of the sun was already soaking into the
pine needles, so that the perfume hung on the air and
skidded down the shafts of light that made diagonal
patterns through the branches. It was sharp and clean,
occasionally mingling with the dank, earthy richness of
the bare earth. We passed a few walkers, but left them
far behind in the wood and soon found that we had the
moor to ourselves, with only the sheep and hardy
Dartmoor ponies for company.

Overhead, two buzzards were circling on the
thermals, mewing to each other, and searching the
ground for the sudden movement that would betray the
location of a possible meal. I think they're fascinating
birds, and could watch them for hours. In the sky,
they're masters of the airways, brushing off attacks from
crows with a disdainful roll of the body, plummetting
from a hundred feet to snatch at prey singled out by
their sharp black eyes. On several occasions, I've been
lucky enough to get quite close to them when they've
been on the ground. There's a nesting pair near the yard
where I stable my horse, Kate, and they often land on a
flat stretch of moor where we practise my dressage tests.
The first time I caught sight of them, I was genuinely
surprised by their size – so much larger than even the
fattest chicken – and when they spread their wings to
glide off to the protection of a hedge top, they passed so
close I could pick out every shade of brown and beige on
the feathers across their four-foot span.

But on our summer ride, there were no such close
encounters. The buzzards kept well clear of us, content
to circle and glide until we were way out of their hunting
ground.

By the time we reached the top of Sheep's Tor, we'd
been climbing steadily from the road for almost half an
hour. The reservoir was now just a slim band of blue
hemmed in by the trees. Away to the right, the roofs of
Sheepstor village shone silver-grey in the sun, and to
our left we could pick out the shapes of even older
homes in a veritable township of hut circles and
enclosures. Obviously, those ancient peoples found this
bit of land just as attractive as the modern-day visitors.

We picked our way carefully over the clitter – small
granite boulders – and boggy streams that criss-cross
the ground, making for the top of Gutter Tor. What an
unglamorous name that is – but then the moor is
covered with an extraordinary collection of labels.
There's the delightfully named Laughter Tor above
Hexworthy; Honeybag Tor near Widecombe; Cuckoo
Rock and Great Gnats Head above Burrator, and even a
Rippon Tor – but no relation!

From Gutter Tor, the moor runs for two miles over
flat, open land known as Ringmoor Down. That
summer, the grass had turned dry and yellow after
weeks of sunshine and when we looked across the great
expanse of corn-colored turf, it shimmered like a prairie
with the heat haze rising in waves making the hills
towards Plymouth ripple like a mirage. I'm told that a
local horse owner used to train his point-to-point racers
on this bit of moorland, and I guess someone must have
told my horse the tale as well. In his youth, Skippy had
been a racing pony and the sight of any flat, open ground
was guaranteed to make him think he was back on the
race track again.

He galloped with all the joy and enthusiasm of one
who lives for the exhilaration of speed. So when I let
him have his head on Ringmoor Down he thundered
across the uneven turf, confident and surefooted. We
flew over the ancient Abbot's Way that took the monks
from Buckfast Abbey to Tavistock, past the cairns that
mark ancient Bronze Age burial sites, and along the
arrow-straight path of a stone row. Not until we got to
the uneven ground above Brisworthy did Skippy make

The clustered buildings of Sheepstor village

any attempt to slow up and then stop. It was undoubtedly one of the most exhilarating rides I'd ever had in my life.

When I got my own horse Kate, some years later, she showed the same enthusiasm to eat up that same ground in an endless, joyous gallop and, if anything, she went even faster. But, nevertheless, it's the sensation of that first gallop that I still remember – stride for stride.

From Brisworthy, our pace was much slower. Not just out of consideration for the horses, though Skippy would have galloped another mile had I let him, but because the ground is pitted and uneven with boulders and stream courses. We were heading for Cadover Bridge, a local beauty spot that straddles the upper reaches of the River Plym. While we were still more than two miles away, we'd been able to locate our goal from the flares of sunlight on car roofs and windows. It's a popular spot for local families since the river runs clean and deep over a shingle bed, forming a series of most attractive natural swimming pools, whilst the surrounding hills provide shelter from the keenest winds turning the whole place into a regular little sun spot.

As we trotted along the river bank, most of the families were settled on the grass eating picnic lunches, and the sight of all that food made Father and me think for the first time of our own stomachs. But lunch was still a good half an hour's ride away so we pressed on, leaving the river behind us, followed the sheep tracks over Wigford Down, and began the homeward run.

We dropped down into the oak woodland on the slopes above another local beauty spot, Shaugh Bridge. Here the Rivers Plym and Meavy meet under the nose of the towering Dewerstone Rock, and you can see the strength of a Dartmoor river at its best. By now, both waterways have forsaken their quiet, shingle reaches to splash and clatter over massive moss-stained boulders in spectacular mini waterfalls and whirling pools of impatient froth.

Beauty spots on the ride : the Dewerstone Rock, Cadover Bridge and near Shaugh Bridge

We could hear the excited cries and laughter of children who were running beside the river and leaping the boulders. The sound carried up through the trees on the still air, but we turned away from the bridge, riding up the Meavy Valley on a narrow track that wound through the tall, sun-streaked trees and past the adventure centre used by the local Boy Scouts. The ground fell away sharply from the path down to the river bed. We could hear the water rushing and gurgling below us, and could trace its course by the flashes of sunlight that sparkled and danced amongst the leafy branches.

Suddenly we spotted a tree that looked distinctly odd and out of place among its sober neighbours. As we got closer, we realised that it wasn't a tree at all – but a beautifully carved and painted totem pole. We looked for Indians – saw none – so rode on through!

A mile further on, below the hamlet of Goodameavy, we left the track through the woods, passed over another attractive stone bridge, and rode along the edge of the road to Clearbrook – and lunch.

The Skylark Pub is used to providing sustenance for riders. They have a small field at the rear of the pub where the animals can be unsaddled and grazed, and wide grassy banks in front. At one-thirty, I thankfully slipped out of the saddle, let the horse nibble on the short, sweet grass, and ordered a pint of orange squash and a pasty. Half an hour later, we were rested and refreshed, ready for the final part of our ride.

This took us over the more familiar ground of Yelverton Golf Course and Roborough Down.

Clearbrook village and the pub where we had lunch, The Skylark ; hunting near Sheepstor

During the last war, Yelverton had been the site of an emergency airfield, and although local farmers have torn up many of the old tarmac runways, to return the land to common grazing, some of the slip roads and aircraft parking bays still remain, and make a perfect parking area for families who drive out from the city of Plymouth to enjoy a bit of fresh moorland air.

That Sunday, the old airfield was packed with people playing football and cricket, flying kites or just sitting in the sun reading the Sunday papers. A few year ago, the Dartmoor National Park did a survey to find out how the visitors used the moor, and they found that something over eighty percent of them never go more than one hundred yards from their cars. Obviously that's how they enjoy Dartmoor, but I hope that one day they're bold enough to step a bit further, and discover a little of what they've been missing.

By now we were into the early afternoon, and just a few miles from home. We took one of the tracks along the wooded common that runs parallel with the River Walkham, from where I could look across the trees to our house. I could see Christopher washing the car in the drive and shouted across the valley to him. On the clear quiet air, the sound carried with ease. He looked in our direction, and waved the chamois leather in greeting. 'Had a good ride?' he bellowed. 'Yes,' I shouted. 'See you soon,' and left him to finish the car.

We rode down through the woods towards Grenofen Bridge, another of those attractive single-arched granite bridges that crop up all over southern Dartmoor. When this one was built early in the 1800s, the stonemasons made it just wide enough to take one cart, and excluded any side walls. Modern cars can just negotiate the narrow track, but a safety-conscious council has added a metal rail along each side.

The lane from the bridge winds steep and narrow, and at the top of Grenofen Hill, we crossed the main Tavistock road, and headed back to the stables, down another long, narrow lane, bordered with fat Devon hedges. The banks were sweet with the smell of honeysuckle and alive with bees and butterflies, whose gentle flight from flower to flower echoed our own steady unhurried pace.

Polly and Skippy tucked into their tea with relish, while Father and I went home to grab the last of the afternoon sun.

As I've been writing this, I've traced that original ride on my old map, enjoying again the sight of Burrator reservoir, the lonely sound of the buzzard and skylark, the sensation of speed, and the pleasure of looking back from Roborough Down across to the distant tors and valleys that I'd been riding over just a few hours before. I trace the route often in my mind, but it's a while since I actually rode it. Sitting here, with the map in front of me, I think perhaps it's time Kate and I found an excuse to take a day off – soon.

Pew Tor and Vixen Tor

One of the main advantages of being able to ride a horse on Dartmoor is that since four legs can carry you further and faster than two, it's possible to reach the quieter, more remote spots on the moor with reasonable ease. Because I ride my horse, Kate, every day when I'm at home, I've been able to build up a network of routes from the stable which offers plenty of scope to keep her fit, and provides me with a kaleidoscope of moorland scenery within which I can enjoy the peace and pleasures of my country life.

Just a mile or so from where I stable the horse at Walkhampton village is Pew Tor, one of the more accessible and picturesque tors on the moor. All through the year, it's a favourite spot for people from the local villages, and Tavistock, to exercise their dogs; and during the summer, it's a regular weekend haunt for families from Plymouth who swarm up its gentle slopes to explore the weird shapes of the granite outcrops on the summit, or to stand for a while taking in yet another of those stunning, panoramic moorland views.

It's a route I often ride. The steady pull from seven hundred to just over a thousand feet above sea level is a good test of Kate's stamina, and the sort of gallop she enjoys. I only have to cross over the small stream that skirts the lower western slopes, and turn her head towards the summit, for her to take a hold of the bit, plunge forward in anticipation of a good gallop and then set off up the grassy track at a thundering pace that sends the wind whistling past my ears. At the top of the hill, we always pause for a few moments: it gives Kate a chance to get back her breath, and me an opportunity to take in the sweep of a view I never tire of. In the far distance, the hills of Cornwall turn purple with the heat haze of summer, but on the clear crisper days of autumn, the light can be so pure that it's possible to trace every field and hedge for miles.

At the foot of the tor, there is a formal pattern of fields in which our friends Mike and Wendy Doidge rear their

On the slopes below Pew Tor with Kate, looking across the stunning panoramic moorland

fine flock of Devon Closewool and Whiteface Dartmoor sheep. A few yards beyond is the unmistakeable roof style of a Devon longhouse where John Hearn, his father, and his father before him have tamed the rough moorland turf into fine grazing.

If you visit John, you have to watch out for his 'geriatric' geese. There are three of them, all bought over eight years ago to fatten for Christmas. But John and his wife got so fond of them that they didn't have the heart to slaughter them so they wander around like family pets, along with the twenty-two-year-old Dartmoor pony and the eighteen-year-old donkey.

From the back of the Hearns' house, Pew Tor looms large and solid and, looking up at it from the farmyard, it's easy to see how it has earned the family nickname of 'The Old Grey Battleship', for that's just what it looks like. Most weekend visitors and dog-walkers are happy to storm the bulk of the 'battleship' and go no deeper into the moor. So Kate and I usually have the moor beyond and behind Pew Tor to ourselves – and that's one of its great attractions.

The ground behind the tor is covered in clitter and we have to pick our way carefully between the sharp edges and overlapping stones and usually follow one of the narrow sheep tracks that run like fine pencil lines all across the moors. From the side of Pew Tor, you can look over towards Princetown and see a different face of Dartmoor. There are no lush green fields or convenient network of roads here. Only the open barren land of Walkhampton Common. The bracken and coarse grass is punctured by a smattering of small tors, old quarries and littered with the remains of hut circles which were the first primitive homes of the moor's earliest inhabitants.

A thin band of ancient oak woodland winds along the basin of the valley, and the occasional break in the trees reveals the secret course of the upper reaches of the River Walkham. At the bottom of Pew Tor, a well-worn track provides a junction – and a choice. Either we go right towards the small hamlet of Samford Spiney, or left – a little deeper into the moor. Invariably, I choose

to go left as the path eventually leads to a place that has become very special.

Within a few hundred yards, the track is littered with large granite boulders again – this time around the base of a small hill, hardly large enough to be worthy of the name tor, but marked on the map as Heckwood Tor. A century ago, when granite was a prime building material, and the protective mantle of the Dartmoor National Park wasn't even a gleam in the government's eye, the granite tors were looked upon as a rich, free source of stone.

Many of the outcrops bear evidence of some blasting and quarrying, though a hundred years of careful repair work by blackthorn and heather have made most of the smaller quarries look almost natural. But at Heckwood, you might easily believe that the stonemasons had just knocked off for lunch and would be back in an hour to finish their work. If you can have a quarrying equivalent of the *Marie Celeste* – this is it. Several large blocks, each weighing a ton or more, are piled on the side of the track, all bearing the clear cylindrical marks of the granite cutters, primitive but effective cutting tools which leave

Remains of granite quarrying ; Vixen Tor

a series of indentations along the edge not unlike the perforations on a postage stamp.

A few smaller rocks were obviously just being prepared for shaping, and in the middle of the quarry sits a lone, magnificent example of the stonemasons' art. It is an enormous block of beautifully 'dressed' granite, the size of a kitchen table, just waiting to take its place in the walls of some elegant building – or, more likely, the Plymouth breakwater which took much of its stone from this quarry. But the granite cutters won't be back after lunch – they won't ever be back again. So the stone sits in glorious isolation and, with its edges clean and sharp, looks uncomfortably out of place next to its rough and ready neighbours. A family of stoats lives in the rocks nearby, and I caught them unawares one summer's day, drowsily stretched out in the sun on the top of the stone – so obviously it has its uses!

At the quarry, the path comes to an end. From there on, Kate and I are back on the coarse uneven turf, heading for our goal, the deep basin lying between the three points of Heckwood, Feather and Vixen Tors. The main road between Tavistock and Princetown is a little more than half a mile away from here as the crow flies, but in this spot, on any day, you might be a million miles from anywhere.

A few years ago, I had to go to New York during the spring on a filming trip. I'd been to the city the year before and found it brash and dark, with too much concrete to be beautiful, too many hang-ups to be comfortable. So the day before flying out from Heathrow, I made a special point of riding to this part of the moor. The land is open and empty, sloping away and down to the black peat and bright green mosses of a small boggy stream, then rising to that weird pinnacle of the sphinx-like rock, Vixen Tor. A small plantation of oak and blackthorn is clustered around the base of Vixen Tor but, apart from that, there's not a single tree or bush in sight as the moor rolls on for acre after empty acre.

On that spring day, I sat in the middle of this quiet oasis, soaking up the view, and the solitude. A single skylark was singing for joy somewhere overhead and a few ponies laconically ripped and munched at the coarse grass. The silence was wonderful, but after a while it made Kate restless. She obviously didn't appreciate the importance of this moment as much as I, so I stored away the view and atmosphere, and rode back to the stable.

A few days later, when black youths in Harlem were throwing bottles at our car and I was surrounded by the poverty and filth of that place, it was good to have my Dartmoor images to relieve the awful reality of the slums. And on many occasions since, it's been extremely useful to be able to momentarily close my mind to an ugly or unhappy situation, switch on that 'inward eye' as Wordsworth called it, and enjoy the quiet solitude of that Dartmoor landscape.

The view from Pew Tor, looking towards Princetown

The Saddle

A viewer from Leicestershire recently sent me a lovely old book, published in 1900 by a firm in Exeter, and called *Dartmoor Illustrated* by T. A. Falcon. It contains one hundred black and white photographs of some of the outstanding features of the moor, along with what it describes as 'some short topographical notes'. Mrs Margery Pickford wrote to say: 'I thought you might like to have this old book, knowing how much you love Dartmoor.' How right she was! Something as ancient and permanent as Dartmoor doesn't change in eighty short years, so the Victorian photographs are as valid now as they were then, and the text more than satisfies the author's intention 'neither to guide nor enlighten – but merely to recall'.

Looking from Cox Tor to Staple Tors, across the Saddle

Mr Falcon's observations make delightful, historically quaint reading, as he has the knack given to so many Victorian travel writers of being able to tame something as wild and spectacular as Dartmoor by couching his descriptions in worthy, pedantic language. But it's because of that unique underplayed style that I take issue with him on one of his descriptions. When talking of the view from Staple Tors, he says merely, 'The view from this tor has much to recommend it.' What an understatement!

I know I've said it many times before, and no doubt this won't be the last, but here on Dartmoor we really do have some of the finest views in England, and from Cox Tor and from Staple Tors, lying a little to the north of the Tavistock–Princetown road, there's one of the best. From a distance, the twin tors are unmistakable as

they're joined by a shallow trough of land known locally as 'The Saddle' with Cox Tor being the cantle and Staple Tors, the pommel.

It takes less than fifteen minutes at a steady pace to walk up the gentle slopes of The Saddle – although I must admit, I usually manage to cover the ground in less than three, as this is one of Kate's favourite gallops. At the top of the hill, we can look down from a vantage point almost fifteen hundred feet high and there are days when it feels as if I'm standing on top of the world. Away to the north through the gateway of Roos Tor and White Tor, lies Petertavy Great Common and, beyond that, the biggest and wildest part of the 365 square miles that make up the Forest of Dartmoor.

I know of people who have lived on the edge of the moor all their lives who won't venture into that part of the forest. They find it overwhelming and frightening –

Storm clouds sweeping in from Staple Tors to Great Mis Tor;
the intriguing silhouette of Staple Tors

while others equally love the raw, untamed hills that offer one of the last areas of wilderness in the British Isles. There are no roads and no signposts for ten miles in a straight line, due north, so it's certainly no place for the casual walker, and not even the seasoned enthusiast should venture in without a map, a compass and the promise of a fine weather forecast.

I know of only one man who could ride into the moor and guarantee he wouldn't get lost. He's Bill Bellamy of Petertavy. As a youth, he was a Moor Man – one of the freelance herdsmen who spent their summers on the moor, grazing huge herds of cattle, moving them day by day to new pastures. He memorised every tor and valley, the location of every bog and river head, and learnt the short cuts through the peat passes – the deep narrow channels that offer safe passage through some of the more treacherous ground.

Bill is now in his seventies and the map is still finely etched on his memory. He's passed some of his knowledge on to his son, Peter, who is Master of the local

foxhounds, and knows the moor better than most. But they're a rare breed.

In contrast, you need no map or compass to enjoy the view from the south side of The Saddle. To the west, Kit Hill stands proud above the Cornish border, dwarfing the hills that surround the towns of Tavistock and Gunnislake. To the east, the hills and tors of the southern moor border the horizon. The dark green bank of conifer plantations just below Sharpitor conceals that most lovely of moorland reservoirs, Burrator. And in the far distance, the white cones that stand stark and incongruous on the skyline, mark the spot of the china clay industry at Lee Moor. In the middle distance, you can just make out the twin towers of the Tamar Bridge, and follow the streak of water that matures from the Tamar to the Hamoaze and, eventually, the sea.

You can watch the weather change from here. I've seen rain falling on Tavistock, while shafts of sunlight have streaked down like divine laser beams on the villages east of Plymouth, with clouds in the centre rolling and jostling each other, torn between soaking the landscape with a heavy downpour or moving aside to let in the sunshine. No wonder the poor weather forecasters can't ever get it right – from The Saddle you can see four different climates in as many miles, and know that half an hour later it will look totally different.

Whatever the time of year, or time of day, the view has something special to offer, whether it's a pattern of cloud shadows scudding across the fields on a summer's evening, or the soft-edged, dreamlike quality of pink sky above purple hills that comes with the autumn mists.

My own favourite moments occur during the early mornings of late summer while the day is still fresh and new. The valleys fill with soft white clouds of mist, rising slowly off the streams and rivers in lazy swirls so that the trees and high ground are isolated, like small islands in an ocean of down. That's when the view becomes almost unreal, as if the whole moor is being born again out of the depths of a witch's cauldron.

The view from Cox Tor always has something special to offer, whatever the time of year or time of day

The Different Faces of Dartmoor

A road winds across the moor; the ancient clapper bridge at Postbridge, and Longford Tor

Conifers near Ponsworthy; a moorland stream which feeds the Burrator Reservoir, and above Dartmeet

An Unlikely Racecourse

It's impossible to walk far on the southern slopes of Dartmoor without, sooner or later, coming across the perfectly formed circles of low granite walls described in Gothic type on the Ordnance Survey map as 'hut circles' and known locally as 'pounds'.

These were the homes of the Bronze Age settlers on the moor, the 'moormen' who built their circular shelters from the granite boulders that were lying all around them, and then enclosed the whole community with a stout wall, to create a barrier and stockade large enough to house their cattle every night, and formidable enough to defend their community against marauding invaders.

One of the largest and most famous pounds on the moor is Grimspound. It holds the flat middle ground between the peaks of Hookney and Hameldown Tors in the direct path of one of the old moorland ways on the hills above Postbridge. It covers just over four acres and contains the remains of twenty-four huts. It's a mysterious, magical place and I defy anyone to stand in the middle of the ring, hear the wind whisper and eddy around the hills and through the valley, and not be touched by its history and atmosphere. I must admit it's a place I like to walk to in the summer when I can feel the warmth of the sun on my back, and the light on my face. I've only been there once during the winter and it gave me the shivers – and not just because it was cold.

They were obviously great builders, those ancient settlers, for they didn't just confine their talents to practical constructions like the huts and enclosures.

Close to a number of settlements, there are ancient 'stone rows', varying in length from a few feet to several hundred yards. For years, historians were baffled by them and offered all sorts of explanations about their use – some less serious than others. There was speculation that they might have been used for gymnastic performances, that they were roads for Druids, had astronomical significance, or were meant to represent soldiers drawn up in battle order. All very picturesque, and if your imagination is colourful enough, quite plausible. But the consensus of opinion is that they were very probably an important feature of burial ceremonies, though as far as I know, no one has ever actually come up with any bones!

One of the most spectacular double stone rows is at Long Ash Hill, just a few yards from the B3357 which leads to Princetown past the stone quarry at Merrivale. It's easily seen from the road, but well worth the effort of walking just a few hundred yards across the moor for a closer look.

I remember coming across it once, more by accident than design. I'd ridden to Princetown with a woman who was doing a sponsored long-distance ride from Land's End to John o'Groats to raise money for the Riding for the Disabled Association. As I've been a Vice-President of that organisation for some years, I was one of several people throughout the country who'd agreed to ride with her for part of the way, to help drum up support and make the journey seem a little shorter with companionship and conversation.

Merrivale stone quarry ; the remains of the Bronze Age village of Grimspound, an exciting and evocative monument

We parted company near Two Bridges, then Kate and I turned for home, taking the shortest, most direct route across the open moor. We rode under the shadow of the tall television mast on North Hessary Tor, skirted around the boggy ground below King's Tor, and struck out for Merrivale. As we came over the brow of a gentle hill, there in front of us was the double row of granite stones at Long Ash. They're not large, probably no more than two or three feet high, and more than one historian has wondered why the builders didn't choose a more impressive group of stones for the row – after all, there's hardly a shortage of material. But perhaps those early men wanted simplicity not grandeur, and that's just what they've achieved. The southern row is eight hundred and fifty feet long, its neighbour has a few stones missing and stops short at five hundred and ninety feet. They stand like sentinels – perfectly straight lines running across the flat moor.

When you stand at the end of of the rows, it's easy to be drawn along them – to walk in mock procession along the route taken by Druids, holy men or whoever, in centuries past. On a horse, it's a little more difficult and, anyway, Kate had already got the scent of home and was anxious to be off. So we galloped along the outside of the rows, being paced, stride for stride, by the perfectly measured stones for almost a quarter of a mile. Had anyone seen us, they might almost have believed in another theory about the origins of the rows – that they were placed there by ancient men to mark the route of a race course!

The stone rows near Merrivale – a prehistoric racecourse?

On Top of the World

If you've ever been into a portrait gallery and felt the eyes of those framed stoics following you around the room, then you'll know exactly what I mean when I say that I sometimes feel it's impossible to travel anywhere on the south-western tip of Dartmoor without the familiar outline of Brent Tor staring down on me from the horizon.

Although the moor is full of hills and high tors, many topped with fascinating irregular granite shapes, the contours tend to curve gently across the skyline in a series of rounded folds and dimples that stretch towards eternity. But Brent Tor is visibly different. It forms an almost perfect triangle, sticking its nose into the air a thousand feet above sea level, with the square outline of a diminutive Norman church perched right on the summit. It just demands to be noticed. When you approach the moor from the south, along the main road from Plymouth to Yelverton, it's a little like driving into a gigantic amphitheatre with Sharpitor and Gutter Tor, Staple Tor and Gibbett Hill encircling from the right, but straight ahead there's the unmistakeable outline of Brent Tor, watching silently from its vantage point more than ten miles away.

When I ride across the flat open plain of Whitchurch Common or over the springy heather of Roborough Down, even climb to the top of Staple Tor and look out across one of the widest, best views in Devon – the little church and its unique hill ease themselves gently into the picture.

Occasionally, something that's attractive to look at from a distance, falls short of expectation when you take a closer look. Happily that isn't the case with Brent Tor. For years, it's been a favourite walking spot for Chris and me. On the coldest days in winter, we've stood on its summit and let the full blast of an east wind blow the cobwebs out of our lives, and on summer evenings, when the shadows run long and purple across the sunlit turf, it's a good place to let the dogs run while we enjoy the mellow end of the day.

The hill is on the northern side of Tavistock on one of the minor roads to Lydford, and just a few paces inside

Brent Tor demands to be noticed

the boundary of the Dartmoor National Park. When you're less than a mile from the hill, it looks even more incongruous than from a distance since the fields all around offer good, flat grazing land, and if you just half close your eyes, you might almost believe that some eccentric had built a pyramid in the middle of a green desert. The climb to the top of the hill is steep enough to set your heart pounding and your legs aching, whether you follow the thin gravel path that meanders the easy way around the hill, or the sheep tracks that dodge in and out of granite boulders in a straight line from top to bottom. And when you reach the summit – if you have any breath left, the view will take it away.

It's a little like standing on top of a living Ordnance Survey map looking at the rooftops of towns and hamlets, and the ribbons of tarmac roads picked out in grey and silver, the deep tucks in the land betraying the courses of the rivers Tavy, Tamar and Meavy, the granite tors running into wooded valleys and, in the far misty distance, the blue strip of the English Channel. No wonder early settlers built their homes on the

SACRED
TO THE MEMORY OF
JOSEPH GLANVILE
OF THIS PARISH, YEOMAN,
WHO DIED THE 30. DAY OF AUG. 1856
AGED 60 YEARS.
...ieve not dear wife it is in vain.
...ear child, forbear to mourn.
...part to meet again.
...hat your glass is run.

Brent Tor's breathtaking view, and the tiny Norman church

sloping fields around the hill, and then fortified the area. From the top of their granite eyrie, they could spot invaders when they were still a day's march away!

The little church, built in 1319, is one of the smallest in the county – just 37 feet long and 15 feet wide. Inside the three-foot thick walls, there are just the barest of essentials, a few rows of wooden pews and a simple altar – the risk of vandalism unfortunately makes any other furnishings impossible. On one summer's evening, we did find the cool, dark interior brightened with a bunch of wild flowers, bluebells and pink campions stuck in a jam jar by one of the windows – obviously someone thought the place needed a little life and colour.

It's such an unlikely spot for a church that there are predictably a number of delightful stories and legends about how it came to be there at all. One says that the builders originally intended to site the church at the bottom of the hill but each night, when the masons went home, the devil came and carried the stones up to the summit, determined to make it as difficult as possible for the parishioners to get to God's house. Another story suggests that the church was built as an act of thanksgiving by a wealthy merchant sailor, whose first sight of land after surviving an appalling storm at sea was the distinctive cone of Brent Tor.

Services in the church are few and far between with occasional weddings or memorial services held by special request. For those who love Dartmoor, it must be good to look forward to eternity knowing that your spirit will always have a home among the rocky crags and windswept heathers, and although the walk up to the church must be a trial for any bride, how marvellous to emerge from the great oak door after the wedding service, stand on the pinnacle of the Tor, look out over the countryside, and know that, on that day above all others, you would have the world well and truly at your feet.

Index

TITLE PAGE *St Michael's Mount*
DEDICATION *The Barbican, Plymouth*
OVERLEAF *Sunset over Appledore*